The Complete Guide to TurboCAD

by
Randall Newton

San Rafael, CA

THE COMPLETE GUIDE TO TURBOCAD

for Windows V3

Project Coordinator	Rob Berry
Cover Illustration and Design	Claude Moens
Book Design	Dale McKinnon and Randall Newton
Page Layout and Index	Dale McKinnon and Randall Newton
Proofreader	Tamara Cartwright and Rob Berry

IMSI
1895 Francisco Blvd. East
San Rafael, CA 94901-5506, USA
Tel (+1) 415-257-3000
Fax (+1) 415-257-3565

IMSI (UK) Limited
IMSI House, Printing House Lane
Hayes, Middlesex, UB3 1AP UK
Tel (+44) 181-581-2000
Fax (+44) 181-581-2200

IMSI France P/L
75, avenue Parmetier
75011 Paris, France
Tel (+33) 1-40-21-24-64
Fax (+33) 1-40-21-24-03

IMSI Australia P/L
Unit 9, 4 Huntley Street
Alexandria, NSW 2015, Australia
Tel (+61) 2-319-7533
Fax (+61) 2-319-7625

IMSI GmbH
Bayerwaldstraße. 46, D-81737
Munich, Germany
Tel: (+49) 89-637-3357
Fax: (+49) 89-637-3358

IMSI South Africa (Pty) Ltd.
P.O. Box 1000
Ferndale 2160. South Aftrica
Tel (+27) 11-792-9944
Fax (+27) 11-792-9952

TurboCAD is a registered trademark of IMSI

ISBN 1-57632-072-3

First Printing, November 1966

Printed in the United States of America

Contents

Introduction

From humble beginnings in the mid 1980s, TurboCAD has grown to become one of the top low-cost CAD (Computer Aided Design) software products. The current version, TurboCAD 3 For Windows, is filled with features that rival much more expensive products. TurboCAD 3 For Windows offers much more than just a comprehensive set of drawing commands. It is now possible to customize the program, to link drawings with files created by other Windows programs, and to extend the capabilities of the program by writing external software programs that use TurboCAD as a drafting engine. The reference manual that ships in TurboCAD 3 For Windows only hints at some of these more advanced features.

Learning to use a software program becomes more difficult as the complexity grows. This book is written with one goal in mind: to enable you to master TurboCAD 3 For Windows as easily as possible.

How this book is organized

This book reveals the features of TurboCAD 3 For Windows in a natural sequence. Chapter One offers a detailed explanation of Computer Aided Design, and why CAD software is in a class by itself.

Chapter Two covers the TurboCAD 3 For Windows "desktop," and how you can modify it to match your preferences. Chapters Three through Six cover the basics of drawing, editing and modifying. (In TurboCAD, editing and modifying refer to making changes to previously drawn objects.) The terms *editing* and *modifying* have differing meanings in TurboCAD 3 For Windows, and will be explained fully as the book progresses.

Chapters Seven through Twelve cover important topics such as dimensioning (adding measurements to drawings), file management, the use of hatch patterns, and specialized drawing techniques. The final chapters of the book cover printing and plotting, and using TurboCAD 3 For Windows drawings in other software programs.

Explanations, exercises, tutorials

Each command and tool in TurboCAD 3 For Windows has its own explanation. Each command is introduced, typical uses are explained, followed by a hands-on sequence showing you how the command works. In some chapters, these hands-on explanations are progressive, and become part of a larger exercise that continues throughout the chapter. In other chapters, the hands-on sequences are separate. When several tools are very close to each other in use (such as the Align tools), a common explanation is given to avoid being redundant.

If you really want to master TurboCAD 3 For Windows, take time to follow the hands-on exercises and tutorials. It is the rare person who can read through a software manual and immediately go to work. Most users need to practice commands and procedures, and become comfortable gradually. As I often tell my clients, it is one thing for your brain to understand a software command, but quite another for your hands to become equally knowledgeable. The exercises and tutorials in this book bridge the gap between brain and hands.

What you need

This book makes a few assumptions about the program in use, the reader's knowledge, and the computer equipment available.

TurboCAD For Windows Version 3

This book is based on TurboCAD 3 For Windows, published by IMSI, Inc. of San Rafael, California. The program has undergone substantial revision from version 2, and this book does not attempt to cover the differences between the two programs or to provide help with any previous version. If you have an earlier version of TurboCAD, an upgrade to the current version is available directly from IMSI.

Windows operating environment

This book assumes no prior knowledge about TurboCAD 3 For Windows or about a specific method of drafting. It does assume that you have a basic familiarity with the Windows operating environment. TurboCAD 3 For Windows ships in two versions, one for Windows 3.1, and another for Windows 95. In particular, you should know the following:

- How to start (or launch) a program;
- What directories and subdirectories are (also known as folders in Windows 95);
- What files are, and how to copy, move or delete them.

The Windows 95 version of TurboCAD 3 For Windows is fully Windows 95 compliant, and both versions comply with the Microsoft Office standard.

Appropriate computer hardware

TurboCAD 3 For Windows requires a computer with these minimums:

- 386 or better CPU (486 for Windows 95);
- 8 MB RAM recommended;
- 30 MB of free hard disk space;
- VGA graphics card or better;
- A CD-ROM drive to install the 32-bit version of TurboCAD 3 For Windows for use in Windows 95 or Windows NT;
- Windows 3.1 or later.

Summary

If you are standing in the aisle of a bookstore reading this introduction, it's decision time. This book will help you become comfortable and productive with TurboCAD 3 For Windows. It offers explanations in real English and exercises that are practical, yet easy to follow. This book will serve you now as you learn TurboCAD 3 For Windows, and later when you need to review a command or other feature.

The Complete Guide to TurboCAD for Windows V3

1

What Is CAD?

Demystifying CAD

Almost all computer owners have a word processing program. They use it often, and find it very helpful. After all, a word processor is a useful tool for a variety of tasks. Computer users realize you don't have to be a professional writer to make good use of a word processor.

But for some reason, many computer users assume CAD (Computer Aided Design) software is just for technical professionals. They don't see themselves using the same software an architect or mechanical engineer uses. Ask a few computer users, and you'll hear a variety of excuses why they don't have a CAD program:

- "Too complex."
- "I don't have any artistic ability."
- "I don't have a use for it."
- "Too expensive."
- "What's CAD?"

All these answers point to the same fundamental problem — CAD is misunderstood.

Good CAD programs don't have to be complex. (Yes, some are. We won't mention names here.) CAD does not require artistic ability. In fact, artistic ability has nothing to do with learning and using CAD software. As for usefulness, few programs are as versatile as a good CAD program.

Having bought TurboCAD, you already know better than to believe CAD is expensive. Yes, there are CAD programs costing thousands of dollars, but they have features only professional engineers, architects and designers need. As for those computer users who do not know what CAD is, please gently enlighten them. After all, there was a time when you also didn't know CAD stands for both Computer-Aided Design and Computer-Aided Drafting.

This guidebook's purpose is to sweep away the clouds of mystery and misunderstanding that have surrounded CAD. If you can write with a word processor, you can draw with TurboCAD.

CAD Is a Versatile Software Tool

Good software should go beyond the simple automation of an intellectual or creative task and provide an opportunity for expanded capabilities. Spreadsheets and accounting software, for example, make it possible for people without training in accounting to do their own financial record keeping. TurboCAD provides a set of tools and an ease of use that allows anyone to create drawings for a wide variety of applications. They are limited only by their design plans and their creativity.

Learn the fundamentals, and you will quickly see that TurboCAD is a versatile software tool. People who never dreamed of buying a drafting table have used CAD for real estate appraisal and sales, facilities planning, and arts and crafts brainstorming. The same software used by architects to design houses is used by storekeepers to plan retail layouts. Sales representatives use CAD software on laptop computers to draw up bid specifications in the field, and police officers prepare accident reports. Home owners are drawing remodeling plans for contractors and inspectors, saving money and communicating their ideas with precision. The list of applications, both professional and amateur, goes on and on.

A computer is a tool kit for the mind, but too many people only have word and number tools in their kit. TurboCAD makes the visual design tool an affordable and practical addition to any computer user's software tool kit. Once you understand how this tool works, you'll find many uses for it.

Learning to Use TurboCAD

For the most part, so far we've been talking about CAD software in general. But this book is specifically about TurboCAD 2D for Windows Version 3. The book's goal is to teach TurboCAD commands in a useful context, not to document capabilities without giving thought to when or where commands can be used.

Most software manuals are reference manuals, they present commands in isolation. By contrast, this is a handbook, where subject matter is presented in context. The Boy Scout Handbook doesn't just document knots, it explains when to use them. That's an example of context. We will be using a similar approach throughout this book.

So, each chapter from here on out will follow the same pattern. New commands will be introduced and briefly explained. A tutorial project or exercise will provide an opportunity to explore the new features. Finally, each chapter ends with a review of the material covered.

Take the time to follow the tutorials and work through the lessons. Your goal should be to move from head knowledge (where you read a description and assume you understand it) to hand knowledge (where you can actually execute a command correctly).

What Makes a Drawing Program a CAD Program?

A variety of software products create visual images, and they can all be lumped into the category of "graphics software." CAD software belongs in this group, as well as a variety of other programs. Several characteristics distinguish CAD software from other types of graphics software. These five elements are:

- Precision and accuracy
- Automation
- Real Scale
- Coordinate Geometry
- Vector Graphics display

Some graphics software products have one or two of these elements, but it takes all five to be a true CAD program.

Precision and Accuracy

CAD is meant to replace manual drafting, so it must meet the standards of those who do drafting work. Part of the standard is mathematical precision. When you draw a line with TurboCAD, the line has an exact length, which the program can calculate to a precision of eight decimal places. Every line, circle, etc., is on a coordinate grid, the exact location of which TurboCAD stores in memory. (More about the coordinate grid later in the chapter).

When drawing by hand, it's easy to be sloppy and let a line go an extra 1/32" or so, or to jiggle the compass when drawing a circle. But such imprecise actions are impossible in TurboCAD. A 12" line will measure exactly 12". Circles are true, angles are exact. Commands known as Snaps allow you to attach one object to another with extreme precision at exact locations.

Automation

CAD programs are designed to automate the manual drafting process, a demanding, labor-intensive task that has seen little automation in its several hundred years of existence. Flip through a textbook on manual drafting and you will see all the details that must be attended to before one can draw a single straight line. The right diameter pencil has to be sharpened in a certain way, the paper must be carefully attached to the drafting table, the T-Square and the triangle placed correctly, a measurement must be taken, construction points placed, and then *finally* a line can be drawn to connect the two points. Now consider drawing the same line in TurboCAD. You only have to install the program once (the equivalent of setting up the drafting table and placing the paper). Line color, line type and line width are already set (or you can change them easily). Select the Line tool, move the cursor to the point where the line is to begin (perhaps using a Snap command for exact placement). Click the left mouse button once, move the cursor to the end of the line and click again. The line is drawn, at the exact length and width, to the exact color and style.

Other graphics software products automate creating graphic images, but only a CAD program automates drafting.

Real Scale

Real scale means that as you draw, you can use the actual dimensions of the object you are representing on the screen, without regard to fitting it on the screen. When drawing a house plan, for example, you draw a 12' wall as a 12' wall, not as a 6" line that represents a 12' wall.

If you have done manual drafting, you can immediately appreciate the advantages of working with real scale. It is no longer necessary to figure out whether to draw your plans at 1/4" = 1' or 1/2" = 6", or whatever. Using real scale is an easier, less intimidating way of drafting, because you focus on your ideas, not on how to make the drawing fit the paper. TurboCAD is flexible, however, and offers the option of drawing at scale, if you prefer to work that way.

If the concept of real scale gives you trouble, perhaps the following exercise will help. Bring the tip of your thumb and first finger together to form a circle. Put it up to one eye and use the circle as a viewing window to look across the room. Can you see anything larger than the hole you're looking through? Of course you can, and you didn't have to calculate how to reduce the chair, the door, the window, and so forth, to fit your viewing window. TurboCAD is a viewing window into your own private universe of design, and that universe can be any size you choose. If you are drawing a 2,000-square-foot floor plan, for example, it will easily fit onto your computer screen.

TurboCAD can easily take your real scale drawings and print them either at a scale that fits the page, or at a user-selected scale. For more information, see Chapter 13: Printing and Plotting.

Coordinate Geometry

When it comes to TurboCAD 2D, Columbus was wrong: the world *is* flat. TurboCAD 2D's world is a simple, flat two-dimensional plane. Everything you draw in TurboCAD 2D will be placed on this plane. (There is one small exception: Blocks can be optionally rotated into a third dimension.)

Every possible location on the plane has a unique address, which can be written in X,Y coordinates. There is only one place (at any one time) in all of TurboCAD's world that can have the address X 1" Y 1". To record both the length of a line and its position on the plane, the only thing TurboCAD needs to know is the coordinates of each end of the line. A line with one end exactly at X 5" Y 5" and the other end at X 11" Y 5" must be exactly 6" long, and must exist at one and only one place in the coordinate plane.

When you use TurboCAD for the first time, the coordinate display is set to show distances in inches, with two decimal places of accuracy. As you move the pointer, the coordinate display at the bottom of the screen shows the X, Y coordinate position of the cursor as it moves across the drawing area. If the cursor is at X 10" Y 6", then the cursor is 10 inches above and six inches right of a location known as the origin point. This location, near the lower left corner of the drawing area, has the coordinate address of X 0 Y 0. All other coordinates are determined by how far they are from the origin point. Using the origin point as a consistent point of reference for coordinate display is known in TurboCAD as *Absolute Coordinates*. Take a look at the drawing showing the origin point and some points and angles near it.

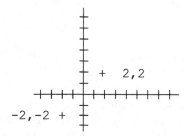

Points (+) defined in Cartesian coordinates

There is more to be learned about coordinate display; this subject will be discussed further in Chapter Five.

Vector Graphics Display

A computer displays information in pixels, the little dots that make up an image on the screen. The more pixels, the higher the resolution of the image and the smoother the image. Paint programs and other types of graphics software are limited by the number of pixels available. Objects in these programs are defined by dots, so detail work can be no finer than the number of pixels available. Paint programs store images as a map of dots, and can't define an image with detail that exceeds the number of available pixels. This is known as *raster graphics,* raster referring to the technology that places the pixels on the screen. Paint programs are sometimes called *device-dependent* software, because the capability to create and reproduce a screen image is dependent on the display resolution in effect on the device in use when the image was created. If you create a drawing on a low-resolution device, then move it to a computer with higher resolution, the image will look grainy or lumpy. The file storing the image lacks the information necessary to display the image at the new, higher resolution. The limited information about resolution also affects printing the image. The higher the resolution offered by the printer, the lower the quality of the illustration if it was created at low resolution.

CAD programs couldn't care less about pixels. Objects in TurboCAD are defined by their geometric characteristics, not by the points of light that display the objects. TurboCAD calculates where the endpoints of lines are to go, for example, and then connects them with pixels to form an image on screen. The program makes this calculation each time the screen is redrawn.

This form of display is called *vector graphics,* since lines and other objects are defined by their geometric properties, which include vectors (headings). It is also know as *device-independent,* since display resolution is not limited by the capabilities of the device on which the image was created. This feature is handy when sharing drawing files with other users, because it doesn't matter what screen resolution is in use by either user. You might use 800x600 resolution on your 13" monitor, and your associate may use 1200x1000 resolution on a 20" monitor. TurboCAD will display your drawing correctly on both monitors, using every available pixel to generate the image.

In a Class by Itself

The use of real scale and vector graphics display, the automation of manual drafting techniques and the use of coordinate geometry sets CAD software apart from all other types of software capable of creating graphic images. Unfortunately, many software designers integrated these capabilities without thinking about how ordinary people would use them. At least that's the way it was before TurboCAD. It combines ease of use with professional CAD power to stand in a class by itself. Starting with the next chapter, we will explore how to become productive using TurboCAD.

2
Fundamental Elements

Getting Started with TurboCAD 3

This chapter will introduce the basic elements of TurboCAD, including:

- Commands and tools
- Objects and entities
- Launching TurboCAD
- The TurboCAD desktop
- Units and scale

The chapter concludes with a tutorial, which introduces the most commonly used commands and tools in TurboCAD.

Commands and Tools

The terms *command* and *tool* are used in this guidebook to describe distinct types of TurboCAD functions.

Command. Commands are functions that start and complete an event. Select All would be an example of a command, because it immediately selects all the objects on the screen and returns TurboCAD to its previous state, expecting no further action from you.

Tool. When you select a tool, you access a special set of functions that are available as long as the tool is active. Some tools remain active until you explicitly switch to another tool. For example, you can activate the Single Line tool and continue to draw lines until you switch to another tool. Other tools, such as Zoom Window, become automatically inactive as soon as you finish using them. As you begin to use the various tools in TurboCAD, notice which category they fall into. You will soon intuitively know whether a tool stays active or functions once and returns to an inactive state.

TIP: *Think of a command like this: You tell TurboCAD what to do, and TurboCAD does it. Think of a tool like this: You ask TurboCAD for the means to perform an action, TurboCAD provides the means, then you perform the action.*

 NOTE: *Occasionally the term "tool" can also be used simply to mean a tool button on the toolbar, or any function accessible using a tool button.*

Commands and tools are accessed either by pressing a button in a toolbar, or by selecting the command from a menu. When a menu command is being specified in this book, the instruction will say "Menu:" followed by the name of the menu and the actual command, separated by a single line. An example would be Menu: Edit|Select All.

Occasionally the use of a command opens up a dialog box, requiring you to adjust settings, choose outcomes, etc., before the command can be executed. The use of dialogs in TurboCAD conforms to contemporary Windows standards. Specific dialogs will be explained as required throughout the book.

Objects and Entities

TurboCAD provides a way to draw a wide variety of *objects* and *entities;* the two terms are not interchangeable. The term *object* is a general term used in this guidebook to mean anything that can be displayed in a TurboCAD drawing. The term *entity* is used in a much more narrow sense, to mean a drawing object created with TurboCAD drawing tools. Entities include single lines, multilines, arcs, circles, polygons, and so forth, as well as construction lines and circles. TurboCAD's entities can be combined together into groups, which are also classified as objects. Other types of TurboCAD objects include bitmaps, metafiles, OLE objects, and symbols.

Entities are independent geometric objects. They would be at home in a geometry textbook, or a manual drafting course. Objects are groups of entities, or other elements of a drawing not easily defined using geometric definitions.

Launching TurboCAD

If you have not already installed TurboCAD, do so now, following the installation instructions in the Introduction. When you are ready to use TurboCAD, select the program using the Start utility in Windows 95 to reach the IMSI folder. If you are using Windows 3.1 or Windows NT, open the IMSI Program Group and click on the TurboCAD icon. The TurboCAD logo screen will appear for a few seconds, to be replaced by the Tip Of The Day dialog. Each time you launch TurboCAD, a usage tip will appear.

Tip of the day

Note the Show Tips at Startup option in the lower left corner of the dialog box. If you do not appreciate seeing a usage tip every time you launch TurboCAD, click on the box to deselect this option.

After the Tip of the Day dialog box, TurboCAD will display the Create from Template dialog box. For now, choose Normal and click OK to continue.

Create from Template dialog

Templates are a special type of drawing file that provide a basis for a new drawing. Templates preserve all of the settings in a drawing, such as unit and scale options, angle conventions, grid settings and colors. If in the future you find yourself using the same settings over and over, take a minute to save those settings as a new template. Use the Save As command (Menu: File|Save As), and select TurboCAD Template from the list of file types.

The TurboCAD Desktop

Once you have chosen the Normal template you will see the TurboCAD desktop with a new, blank drawing. The next illustration shows the basic components of the TurboCAD desktop that appears on your screen.

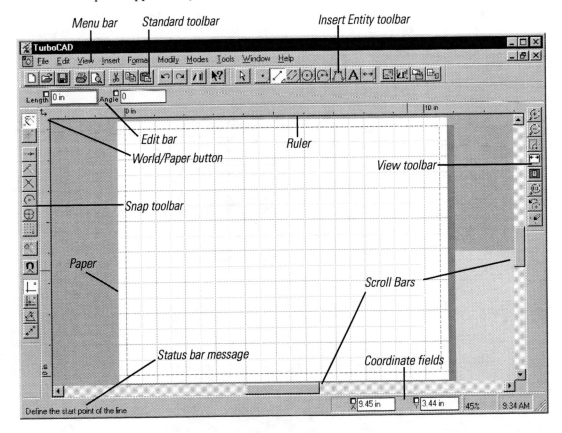

TurboCAD desktop

Here are brief descriptions of the various elements of the screen. The TurboCAD tutorial and help system contain additional information on the desktop elements. Most of these elements are standard Windows features.

Menu Bar. Click on the menu names on the menu bar to access TurboCAD's commands.

Toolbars. Toolbars provide a convenient alternative to the menu system. Your screen is now displaying four toolbars: the Standard and Insert Entity toolbars at the top of the screen, and the Snap and View toolbars on the left and right sides of your screen, respectively. Clicking on any of the buttons on the toolbars will start a TurboCAD command.

✔ *Tip: TurboCAD tools are equipped with tool tips, small yellow rectangles that briefly describe the tool. To see a tool tip, place the mouse cursor on the tool and leave it there briefly.*

Scroll bars. Your drawing can be larger than what you see on the screen. By clicking in the scroll bars, you can "scroll" to a different view of your drawing. Click on the arrow to scroll a small amount. Hold the mouse cursor over the "thumb" of the scroll bar (the rectangle in the middle of the bar) and drag it to move through your drawing. Click in the area between the thumb and the arrow to scroll a larger amount.

Paper. The Paper, the large white rectangle in the middle of the screen, shows you how your drawing will be laid out on the page when printed. You don't have to draw on the Paper; you can draw anywhere in the drawing space. The pattern of horizontal and vertical lines on the Paper is the grid, which marks exact locations in the drawing.

Ruler. The Ruler gives you feedback about the size and position of objects in your drawing. Notice that the unit of measure on the ruler is inches. This is the Normal template's default setting for measurement. *Default* means that if you don't make a choice, the program makes the choice for you. The ruler must display some sort of measurement, so to start with, it displays inches.

Edit Bar. Use the Edit Bar to draw and edit using numeric values such as lengths and angles. For example, you could tell TurboCAD to draw a line exactly two feet long, at a 45 degree angle.

Coordinate Fields. Use the Coordinate Fields at the bottom of the screen to specify a point in the drawing space by its exact coordinates.

Status Bar message. This message area provides a brief message describing the currently active tool, or instructions about how to perform the next step in a drawing or editing process.

World/Paper Button. This button, in the upper-left corner of the ruler, lets you switch the ruler between World space units and Paper space units of measurement, explained in the next section. When using the Normal template there will be no difference. Using another template, such as dboard.tct, there will be a visible difference in the ruler increments. The two arrows represent World units, the sheet of paper represents Paper units.

Units and Scale

There are two distinct "spaces" in TurboCAD : World space and Paper space. The units in World space apply to the real-world objects you draw. The units in Paper space apply to the paper on which your drawing will be printed. Scale in TurboCAD refers to the ratio of

Paper units to World units. A scale of 3/16" = 1', for example, means that an object 3/16" long in your drawing is modeling a real-world object that is one foot long.

Think of World space as the place where you draw objects at their actual sizes. If you are drawing a garage door, you draw it 12' wide. Think of Paper space as the place where your drawings shrink to fit onto a piece of paper. TurboCAD automates this shrinking process, so you don't have to constantly juggle real-world distances and their printed equivalents.

Normally the coordinate system, the ruler and the grid all show units in World space. You can switch to Paper space by clicking the World/Paper button. The Units and Scale property sheet (found in the menu at Tools|Units and Scale) contains options for setting the drawing scale and for controlling the display of linear units. These features will be discussed in detail in Chapter Four. Normally you will use TurboCAD's built-in templates to set up drawing space when you start a new project. The Units and Scale property sheet is for cases when you want to set up your units and scale manually, so we can bypass a detailed discussion for now.

Cursors and Crosshairs

In addition to the normal cursors provided by Windows (such as text insertion and the selection arrow), TurboCAD provides a separate cursor that appears in the drawing space when a draw command is active. By default, it is a small cross. An optional full-screen crosshairs is also available. To switch between the small cross and the larger crosshairs, use the Menu: View|Crosshairs command. The larger version is useful for lining up objects and comparing distances using the ruler.

Selecting the drawing cursor is a matter of personal preference. Some experienced users prefer the large crosshairs, some prefer the small cross. Try both styles and see if you have a preference for day-to-day work.

Create a Simple Drawing

Take a minute now to draw a few simple shapes to represent the start of a simple floor plan. This will provide an opportunity to use several fundamental drawing commands.

1. Before you start, make sure that all the snap modes are turned off. (Snaps are explained in the next section.) Check the Snap toolbar on the left side of the screen and make sure that the No Snap button is highlighted.

No Snap tool

2. Next, choose the Single Line tool from the Insert Entity toolbar. (Or choose Insert|Line|Single from the menu).

Single Line tool

3. Now place the cursor in the bottom left portion of the drawing area and click. By clicking you have defined the starting point of a line. As you move the mouse around, you will see a rubber band line connecting your cursor to the starting point.

Tɪᴘ: *Remember, if you are confused about what to do next in a command, read the status line at the bottom of the screen.*

4. Move the cursor to the upper right, and click near the top right edge of the paper, to finish the line.

Stop and think about what was just accomplished. You drew a line across the top of the paper, more or less of an arbitrary length. If this were to be one wall in a floor plan, does the line represent the right length of the wall? Does the line lay at the right angle in the drawing? Unless you were very careful, have a steady hand and a sharp eye, the answer to both questions is probably "No." Just drawing a single line, without any extra help from the program, is not the best way to create a precise line to represent an object.

Snaps Ensure Accuracy

TurboCAD features several *snap mode* commands. Snap commands allow you to draw and edit with accuracy. Two of the most commonly used snap mode commands are Snap to Grid and Vertex.

Snap to Grid (left) and Snap Vertex tools

When Snap to Grid is active, the drawing cursor can lock onto (or "snap" to) any intersection on the drawing grid (the pattern of intersecting blue lines that you see on the Paper in the center of the drawing area.) The Vertex snap allows the drawing cursor to lock onto any endpoint of an existing line.

When a snap command is turned on, it stays active until you either click its icon to shut it off, or click on the "no snap" icon at the top of the toolbar. More than one snap can be active at the same time.

Use Snap to Grid in the following steps to redraw the first lines of the floor plan with greater accuracy. First delete the existing line, then draw again.

Delete Line

1. Click the Snap to Grid tool in the Snaps toolbar.
2. Click the Select tool in the Insert Entity toolbar (above the drawing area).

Select tool

3. Click on the line in the drawing. The line should then be enclosed in a selection rectangle.

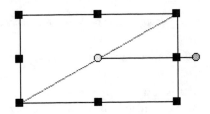

Line enclosed inside selection rectangle

4. Press the <Del> key: The line disappears.

Tip: *Once an object has been selected like this, you can delete it, move it, copy it, scale it or rotate it using a wide variety of techniques.*

Using Flyout Toolbars

You are now going to use a flyout toolbar to choose the Multiline drawing tool. Flyout toolbars are toolbars that "fly out" when you hold the mouse button down while the cursor is over a tool button. Tool buttons that contain flyouts are marked by a small yellow rectangle in their lower-right corner. In this exercise use a flyout toolbar from the Insert toolbar.

1. Position the cursor over the Single Line tool.

2. Hold down the left mouse button. Don't let go of the mouse button until the flyout toolbar appears. It will look like this:

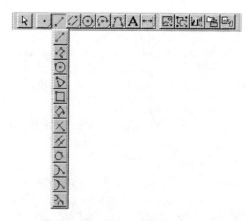

Flyout toolbar from the Single Line tool

3. Click on the Multiline tool.

Multiline toolbar icon

The Multiline tool is now activated, so that you can draw with it. It will remain active until you choose another tool.

 NOTE: *Notice that the button on the Insert toolbar, where the Single Line tool was, now displays the Multiline tool.*

1. Select Menu: View|Crosshairs to switch to a full-screen crosshairs.
2. Move the crosshairs to the upper left corner of the Paper. Click on the lower left corner of the first grid square inside the margin at this location. The ends of the crosshairs should line up at 1/2" on the top ruler.
3. Move the crosshairs straight to the right until the crosshairs line up at 10" on the top margin. Click once at this location, placing the end of the line on the lower left corner of the grid square, just inside the top right corner of the margin lines.

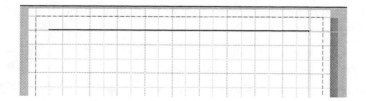

First line drawn using Multiline

Using the Coordinate Fields

Draw the next line of the rectangle using the Coordinate Fields. You'll do this by typing the exact coordinates of the endpoint of the second line. The first endpoint of the line has already been established, because the Multiline tool assumes you are drawing continuous, connected lines.

1. Press <Ctrl>+<R> to activate the Coordinate Fields (bottom right corner of the desktop).
2. Type 10 in. into the X box.
3. Press the <Tab> key to advance to the Y Coordinate Field and type 0.5 in.
4. Press <Enter> to accepts the contents of the fields. TurboCAD places the next line at precisely 10" on the X (horizontal) axis and 1/2" on the Y (vertical) axis. A small diamond marks this point.

Using the Edit Bar

Draw the next line by specifying the length and angle of the line in the Edit Bar. The line will be 9 1/2" long, going straight left from the endpoint of the second line.

1. Press <Ctrl>+<E> (or <Tab>) to activate the Edit Bar (top left portion of the desktop, just below the Standard toolbar).
2. Type -9.5 in. into the Length field. Be sure to use the <Minus> key on the keyboard, *not* the <Minus> key on the numeric keypad.
3. Press the <Tab> key to move to the Angle field, then type 0. The Edit bar should now look like this:

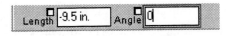

Edit bar showing -9.5 and 0 in fields

4. Press <Enter> to accept the contents of the Edit Bar fields.

TurboCAD draws a line 9 1/2" long, straight left from the end of the second line. Now draw one more line to create a rectangle.

1. Move the crosshairs up to the starting point of the first line. Click on the endpoint to draw a line and close the rectangle.
2. Click on the Select tool in the Insert Entity toolbar, to end drawing mode.

You have now drawn a simple rectangle using the Multiline tool (found using a flyout toolbar), the Snap to Grid tool, the Coordinate Fields, and the Edit Bar. These different features represent the basics of entity placement in TurboCAD. These tools and commands will be used often throughout the rest of the book.

Draw a Rectangle

TurboCAD offers a variety of single line tools, visible when you use the flyout toolbar. We will explore all features in upcoming chapters. For now we will draw one more rectangle, but this time will use the rectangle tool instead of a line tool.

The Rectangle tool enables you to create a rectangle by defining two diagonally opposite corners. Rectangles created this way are oriented orthogonally (sides are true vertical and true horizontal), although they can subsequently be rotated using editing tools.

The existing rectangle on screen, drawn from four separate lines, will represent the exterior of the perimeter walls. The new rectangle will represent the interior of the same walls. To increase accuracy, increase the number of squares in the grid.

1. Select Menu: Tools|Grid. Click on Advanced Grid tab. The Drawing Setup dialog appears.

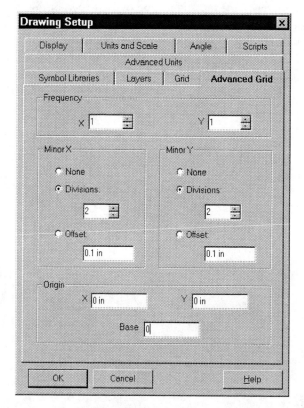

Drawing Setup/Grid Settings dialog

2. Look for the Frequency settings. Click the lower selection arrow for both X and Y, changing each to 1.

The Frequency setting is used to alternate visible with invisible grid lines. By setting Frequency to 1, every grid line will be visible. If we had left Frequency at 2, every other grid line would have been visible.

 Note: Snap to Grid will snap to any grid intersection, visible or invisible.

3. Click the Grid tab. Notice how the grid preview in the dialog changes to a denser grid.

4. Click on OK.

5. Move the cursor to the Multiline tool in the Insert Entity toolbar.

6. Hold down the left mouse button. Don't let the mouse button up until the flyout toolbar appears.

7. Drag the cursor down the column to the fifth tool, the rectangle, then let up on the mouse button. The rectangle tool will appear in the toolbar.

8. Move the cursor to the top left portion of the Paper, inside the existing rectangle. Using the Coordinate Fields as a guide, click on the grid intersection at **X .75 in.** and **Y 7.25 in.** to set the top left corner of the rectangle.

9. Move the cursor toward the bottom right corner of the paper. Click on the grid intersection at **X 9.75 in.** and **Y .75 in.** to complete the rectangle.

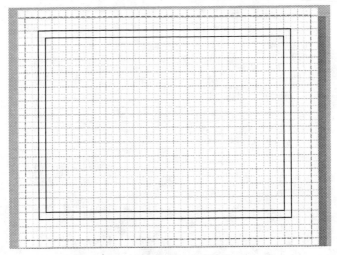

Second rectangle completed

Save the Drawing

It is always a good idea to save your work often. The Save function in TurboCAD follows Windows procedures. The first time you use the Save command in each project, a standard dialog opens. You can specify the drawing name, as well as the disk and directory for storage. One logical place to store this drawing would be the TurboCAD drawings folder. Take the time now to save this drawing if you would like to use it again. It will not be needed for any other tutorials in this book.

If You Make a Mistake

One of the important things to keep in mind as you begin drawing and editing is that nothing is written in stone. TurboCAD allows you to undo your previous drawing command, as well as several of the commands that preceded it. The Undo and Redo buttons are located on the Standard toolbar.

Undo Button

Redo button

Take a few minutes to experiment with the other single-line drawing options in addition to Line, Multiline and Rectangle. Feel free to draw, delete, or save as you prefer. If you feel adventurous, try to use some of the Snap Mode commands not yet introduced.

3

The First Law of CAD

Never Draw the Same Object Twice

As described in Chapter 1, CAD programs use the principles and elements of geometry to create objects. In this chapter you'll construct a geometric puzzle that has baffled generations of math students. Drawing it will familiarize you with more TurboCAD features, and help you gain an understanding of when to modify existing views and functions. The exercise will also demonstrate TurboCAD's keen accuracy, which will enable you to solve the puzzle.

The Extra Square Inch

The problem is simple to set up; try it using pencil, paper and scissors before you draw it in TurboCAD. Draw and cut out two copies of Polygon A and Polygon B, using the dimensions shown. (Or photocopy the next page twice and cut out the polygons. The figures will be smaller, but proportionally correct.)

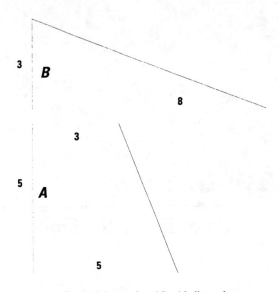

Puzzle Polygons A and B with dimensions

Arrange the four polygons into a square, aligning the outside corners of the objects. There is no need for overlapping.

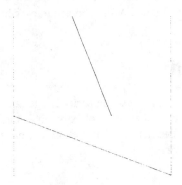

The four pieces arranged into a square

Next, arrange the same four polygons into a rectangle, as shown. Do not overlap the objects. Align them using the outside corners, so that the outside boundary is closed.

The four pieces arranged into a rectangle

When arranged into a square, the area is 64 square inches (8" x 8" = 64 square inches). But when these same polygons are arranged into a rectangle, the area is 65 square inches (5" x 13" = 65 square inches.) Why? Where does the extra square inch come from? The solution is at the end of the chapter—no fair jumping ahead! Draw the puzzle in TurboCAD to see the solution.

New Features in This Exercise

The following new features and procedures will be introduced in this exercise:

- Change Paper scale and display
- Change the on-screen view
- Window selection of objects
- Create a group from individual objects
- Creating, saving and using symbols
- Flipping objects
- Moving an object's reference point

Preparation for Drawing

The standard presentation of the desktop and settings in TurboCAD may not always be right for a particular project. As you become more familiar with TurboCAD and start using it for your own work, you will need to consider the layout of the screen and the status of some of the program's basic settings for each project. Many times you can use the default screen layout and settings, but sometimes you will want to make changes before you draw.

For this exercise, you will modify the TurboCAD defaults for paper size, drawing scale and groups.

By asking yourself questions about the project you wish to undertake, you will better know which settings need to be changed, if any. In the case of our puzzle, you may be wondering when to change the paper space.

Consider what needs to be done. You need enough room to draw the two polygons and then to place four copies of each polygon (two for the square, two for the rectangle) on-screen at the same time. You could draw outside the boundaries of the Paper, but you would lose the ability to snap to the grid. And, you might find drawing outside the boundaries of the Paper distracting, even if you used an alternate means of drawing (such as typing coordinates or distances, as demonstrated in Chapter Two.) A simple solution is to increase the size of the Paper.

The reasons for modifying the Create Group default settings will be explained below, when the Create Group command is introduced.

Modify Paper Space

The following steps prepare the drawing area for the project.

1. Select Menu: Tools|Drawing Setup. A dialog will appear. Select the Units and Scale tab if it is not already selected.

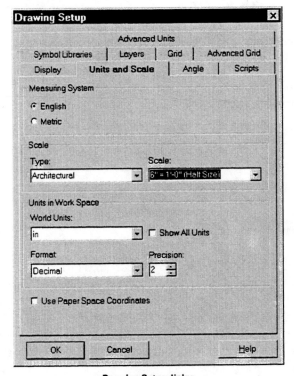

Drawing Setup dialog

2. In the Scale section, click the selection arrow for Scale. Click on "6" = 1'-0" (Half Size)" as displayed above.

3. Make sure "Use Paper Space Coordinates" is not selected. Click on OK.

4. Select Menu: Tools|Program Setup. A dialog will appear. Select the Desktop tab if it is not already selected.

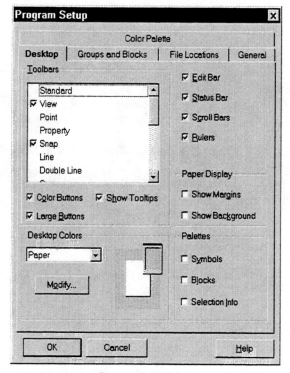

Program Setup dialog

5. Deselect both Paper Display settings (Show Margins and Show Background), as illustrated above. Click OK.

Draw Polygon 'A'

Draw the first piece of the geometry puzzle.

1. Click the Zoom Extents tool in the View toolbar (right side of screen).

Zoom Extents tool icon

2. Click on Grid in the Snaps toolbar (left side of screen).

Grid Snap tool icon

3. Click on Single Line in the Insert Entity toolbar (top of screen).

Single Line tool icon

4. Move the drawing cursor to the top left portion of the paper, and click on a grid intersection to start a line.

5. Using the grid and Edit Bar as a reference, draw a 5" line straight down the sheet. Each thicker blue line of the grid represents a distance of 1".

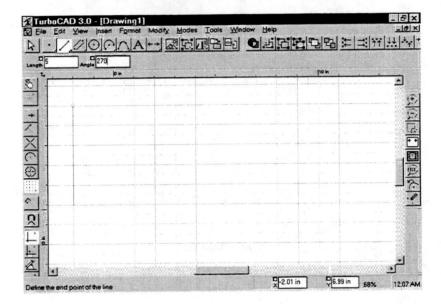

Drawing the first line

6. Draw the next line by clicking where the first line ended, moving 5" to the right, and clicking to finish the line.

7. Move the drawing cursor back to the beginning of the first line. Click to start a new line. Move the cursor 3" to the right, and click to finish the line.

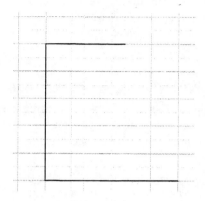

Second and third lines drawn

8. Draw a fourth line to close the polygon.

Selecting Objects

The next step is to identify the four lines as a single group. This will make it possible to deal with the objects as a single polygon instead of four individual lines.

The first step in creating a group is to select the objects to become members of the group. The Select tool (in the Insert Entity toolbar) is used to select the objects. The drawing cursor changes to a selection arrow cursor (similar to the selection cursor used in many other Windows programs). When you click on the object to be selected, it is highlighted on screen. The object is now in Select Edit mode.

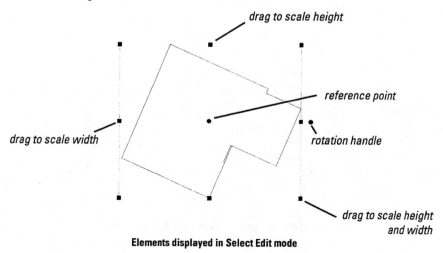

Elements displayed in Select Edit mode

In Select Edit mode, the selected objects are bounded by a *selection rectangle* that has handles on each corner and at the midpoint of each side. At the center of the selection rectangle is the *reference point,* which is connected to the *rotation handle,* located just outside of the selection rectangle.

TIP: *You can get information about a selected object by choosing Menu: View/Selection Info.*

There are three ways to move a selected object: "picking it up" by its reference point, dragging it by its reference point, and "simple dragging" (dragging by any point within the selection rectangle other than the reference point).

TIP: *Dragging by the reference point is technically considered OLE Drag and Drop. OLE is a Windows term that means Object Linking and Embedding. When you drag by the reference point, you can not only drag the object across the drawing screen, but to another TurboCAD drawing or to another Windows program that supports OLE in Client mode.*

In most cases, the most convenient and accurate way to move a selected object is to click on the reference point, then define a new location for the reference point. The object moves with the reference point. If a Snap command is active, the reference point will snap to an endpoint (or a grid point, etc.) as required.

An advanced form of this technique is available (and will be used shortly): the reference point is relocated on the selected object before the object is moved. This feature will come in handy when you organize the polygons to form the square and the rectangle.

1. Click on the Select tool in the Insert Entity toolbar.

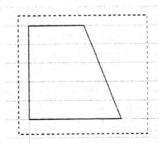

Select tool icon

2. Move the cursor to a location above and left of the polygon. Click and drag, creating a dotted-line selection window. Drag the cursor down and right, drawing the window completely around the polygon.

A selection window drawn around the polygon

Creating Groups

The Menu: Format|Create Group command is used to combine selected objects into a group. The drawing objects can be entities such as lines and circles, non-geometric objects inserted into the drawing, or other groups. TurboCAD treats a group as a single object for the purposes of selecting and editing. Identifying each polygon as a group will make it easier to rotate, flip, and place the polygons to form the square and rectangle. The procedure will mimic the way the square and rectangle are created by hand using cutouts.

From the menu, select Tools|Groups and Blocks to access the Groups and Blocks dialog.

Groups and Blocks dialog

Each group you designate in a drawing can be named. This is a handy feature when creating a complicated drawing with many groups. Each group can be named individually, or the Group Name Prefix command can generate group names. If, for example, we were creating 12 polygons instead of two, the Group Name Prefix could be set to *Poly*. The first group to be named would be *Poly 1*, the second would be *Poly 2*, and so on. The @ symbol in the group name prefix (see Groups and Blocks dialog, above) is the placeholder for the number to be assigned by TurboCAD.

If you intend to name each group you create, but want to assign the names yourself, check the Prompt For Name item in the Groups dialog. When this feature is active, TurboCAD will prompt you for a name every time you create a group. You can accept the name TurboCAD provides or change it.

Groups can be named; so can symbols (introduced in the next section) and blocks (introduced in Chapter Nine). In this exercise we will name the objects only when they are saved as symbols, to avoid redundancy.

1. With the polygon selected, summon the Create Group dialog with the Tools|Groups and Blocks menu command.

2. Deselect both the Generate Group Names and the Prompt For Name options, as illustrated in the Program Setup|Groups and Blocks dialog above. Click OK to finish.

3. Select Menu: Format|Create Group. The selection rectangle and the objects will appear to blink. There is no other visible sign that the command has been performed.

If you want to test that the lines of the polygon are now a group, click anywhere in the drawing area to deselect the polygon, then click on any line of the polygon. All four lines will highlight, and one selection rectangle will appear.

Creating and Using Symbols

A symbol is a pre-drawn shape available for repeated use. Symbols are one of the most important and versatile features of any CAD program. They are also known as blocks or components in other CAD products. Symbols are used to depict objects that will be used over and over, from drawing to drawing. Architects, for example, will purchase and/or create symbols to represent design elements such as doors, windows and furnishings. Mechanical engineers and machinists use symbols to represent screws, bolts, and other common items.

Collections of symbols are known as *symbol libraries*. Symbol libraries make it easy to use any of the thousands of standard drawing components available for TurboCAD 3 for Windows or TurboCAD Designer. Any Windows folder that contains TurboCAD drawings can be used as a symbol library.

Symbols help the CAD user obey The First Law of CAD: *Never draw the same object twice.* If you find yourself drawing an object (or the same object at a different scale) more than once, save it as a symbol or a block. The sooner the better.

There are times when you should save repeated objects as symbols, and times when they should be saved as blocks. A complete discussion of this topic is found in Chapter Nine.

In most CAD programs, symbols behave as one object, the way a group does. In TurboCAD, this is also true, with one big *if*. TurboCAD symbols will behave as a single object *if* the entities that make up the symbol were linked as a group before it became a symbol. If the entities in the symbol were not grouped before being saved as a symbol, then any copy of that symbol placed into a drawing will be a collection of independent entities. Since it is possible to "explode" a group (change it from one object back into components), it is generally better to group entities before saving them as a symbol.

TurboCAD 3 for Windows and TurboCAD Designer are special among CAD programs in that *any* saved drawing can be used as a symbol. In other CAD programs, symbols are created and saved as a separate type of file. This feature provides extra flexibility, because you can insert an entire drawing as a symbol if needed.

IMSI, the publisher of TurboCAD, sells collections of symbols for the most common drafting applications. If you intend to use TurboCAD professionally and wish to save time and money, you should consider purchasing one or several ready-made symbol libraries. Why reinvent the wheel? To get you started, some symbols have been included with TurboCAD.

Saving the First Polygon as a Symbol

Any TurboCAD drawing can be a symbol. To create your own symbol library, all you really need to do is save all the drawings that comprise the library into a single Windows folder (Windows 95) or subdirectory (Windows 3.1 and Windows NT). When you want to create a new symbol on-the-fly, as we do in the this exercise, you can drag objects from a drawing into the Symbol palette. This gives you the added flexibility of saving only part of an existing drawing as a symbol.

Each symbol in the library appears in the palette, with a thumbnail view of each object. If you have several libraries of symbols (each stored in a separate folder or subdirectory), you can add or delete them from the symbol library palette with the Menu: Tools|Symbol Library command.

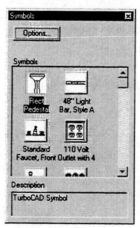

A typical symbol library palette, with several symbols visible

1. If the first polygon is not selected, click on it with the Select tool.

2.   Select the Menu: View|Symbol Library command. The symbol library palette appears on-screen. Reposition it, if you like, as you would any floating window or palette in Windows, by dragging its title bar.

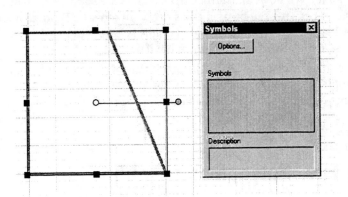

An empty symbol library palette next to the selected polygon

3.   Click and hold on the polygon's reference point (the circle in the middle of the selection rectangle) until the cursor changes to a four-directional pointer. Drag the polygon into the open area of the palette and release the mouse button.

4.   The Save Symbol As dialog appears.

5.   Click on File Name and type Puzl-A.

6.   Click on the Save button. The Summary Info dialog will appear.

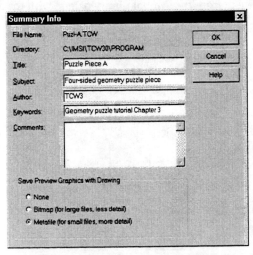

The Summary Info dialog, with details filled in

7.   Click on the text box for each section, typing the following information:

Title: Puzzle Piece A

> Subject: Four-sided geometry puzzle piece
> Author: (Your name)
> Keywords: Geometry puzzle tutorial Chapter 3
> Comments: Leave blank or fill in as you wish

8. Under Save Preview Graphics with Drawing, make sure Metafile is selected.

9. Click the OK button to save. The dialog disappears, and the symbol appears in the symbol library palette.

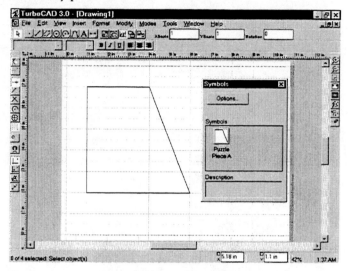

Symbol library palette showing "Puzzle Piece A" symbol

 Tıp: *When moving and rotating objects in TurboCAD, sometimes stray bits of color will stay on the screen after an object moves. You can press function key <F5> at any time to refresh the screen and remove these stray pixels. You may also click the redraw button on the Zoom toolbar.*

Creating the Second Puzzle Piece

Follow the steps below to draw, group, and save the second puzzle piece as a symbol.

1. Click on the Single Line tool in the Insert Entity toolbar.

Single Line tool icon

2. Make sure the Grid tool is selected in the Snaps toolbar.

Grid Snap tool icon

3. In an open area of the drawing screen (move the symbol library pallet and/or use the scroll bars if necessary), click on a grid intersection and draw a line 3" straight down (-90 degrees in the Edit Bar).

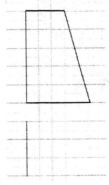

First line of second puzzle piece is a 3" vertical line

4. Connecting to the bottom of the first line, draw a horizontal line 8" long.

5. Draw a third line that closes the polygon, creating a triangle.

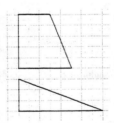

Completed triangle next to first polygon

6. Click on the Select tool icon, and draw a selection window around the triangle.

7. Select Menu: Format|Create Group. The lines of the triangle are now one group.

8. Select the reference point, holding down the mouse button until the four-directional pointer appears. Drag the triangle/group into the symbol library palette.

9. The Save Symbol As dialog appears.

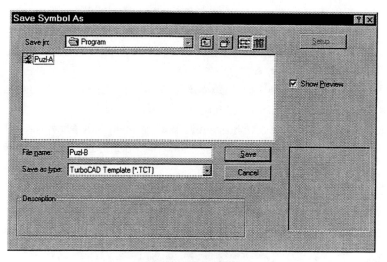

Save Symbol As dialog

10. Type Puzl-B as the file name, and click on the save button.

11. The Summary Info dialog will appear.

Summary Info dialog for Puzzle Piece B

12. Click on the text box for each section, typing the following information:

    Title: Puzzle Piece B

    Subject: Four-sided geometry puzzle

    Author: (Your name)

    Keywords: Geometry puzzle tutorial Chapter 3

    Comments: Leave blank or fill in as you wish

13. Under Save Preview Graphics with Drawing, make sure Metafile is selected.

14. Click the OK button to save. The dialog disappears, and the symbol appears in the symbol library palette. Press <F5> to refresh the screen if necessary.

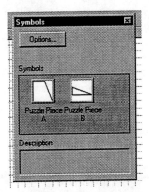

Revised symbol library palette showing both puzzle pieces

Assembling the Puzzle

The pieces have been defined, now it is time to assemble the puzzle and look for the solution to the mystery of the extra square inch. In the steps below, you will start by erasing the objects now on screen, then place the symbols as needed to form the complete puzzle.

When a symbol is placed in a drawing, it appears highlighted with a selection rectangle. The reference point is the symbol's handle, and can be used to place the symbol accurately. If any snap command is active, the reference point will be the part of the symbol that snaps into position. To simplify accurate placement, the reference point will be moved from the center to a corner on each piece. The corners will line up with the grid, allowing for a tight, accurate fit—and to make sure there's no cheating!

Place the First Puzzle Piece

1. The Select tool should still be active. If not, click on the Select tool in the Insert Entity toolbar.

2. Draw a selection window around both puzzle pieces on the Paper. When selected, press the <Delete> key.

3. Drag and drop a copy of Puzzle Piece A (from the symbol library palette) into the drawing.

4. Press the <Ctrl> key and move the selection cursor onto the reference point. When the selection arrow changes to a hand holding a reference point, click the mouse button to "pick up" the reference point.

5. Move the hand cursor to the upper left corner of the polygon, and click directly on the corner. The reference point will move to this new location.

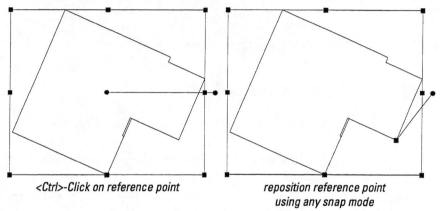

<Ctrl>-Click on reference point

reposition reference point
using any snap mode

Before-and-after example of moving the reference point

6. Keep the cursor on the reference point, and it will change to the four-directional pointer. Click to select the reference point, move the cursor to a point on a grid intersection in the top left portion of the screen and click again to place the reference point.

7. Click anywhere on the Paper to deselect the symbol. Press <F5> to refresh the screen if necessary.

Rotating a Selection

Next a second copy of Puzzle Piece A is placed in the drawing. This second copy needs to be turned upside down before being placed next to the first piece. A rotation command will be used in this example.

An object must be selected before it can be rotated. The selected object always rotates around the reference point. Results of a rotation command will vary depending on the location of the reference point. If the reference point is in the center of the object, the object will stay in the same relative location, but "spin" around the reference point. If the reference point is on a corner, the entire object will rotate on that corner, in effect moving the object to a different location.

For a practical example of the importance of the reference point, place a pencil on a desk. Hold it in the middle with thumb and finger and turn it 90 degrees. Keep thumb and finger pressed against the desk as you turn the pencil. Notice how the center of the pencil stays in the same location. Now hold one end of the pencil and again turn it 90 degrees. Be sure to keep thumb and finger pressed against the desk. This time the pencil seems to jump to a new location.

TIP: *Because rotation is always in relation to the reference point, some interesting effects are possible. The reference point can be moved to a location away from the object, and then rotated. For example, you could use the Snap to Arc Center command to locate a reference point at the center of a circle, then "orbit" the selection around that point.*

TIP: *To restore the reference point to its original location, deselect and reselect the object.*

Place and Rotate the Second Puzzle Piece

1. The Select tool should still be active. If not, click on the Select tool in the Insert Entity toolbar.
2. Drag and drop a copy of Puzzle Piece A (from the symbol library palette) into the drawing, to the right of the first piece.
3. Highlight "0" in the Rotation field of the Edit Bar by pressing <Tab> twice. Type 180 and press <Enter>.

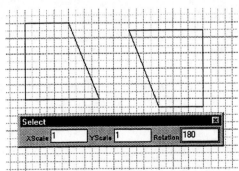

Edit bar shows 180 degrees in the rotation field

4. Press the <Ctrl> key and move the selection cursor on to the reference point at the center of the symbol. When the cursor changes to the hand, click on the reference point.
5. Move the hand cursor to the upper left corner of the polygon, and click directly on the corner. The reference point will move to this new location.

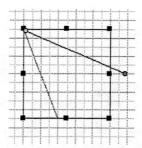

The reference point has been moved to the upper left corner

6. Keep the cursor on the reference point, and it will change to the four-directional pointer. Drag and drop the reference point onto the top right corner of the first symbol.

7. Click anywhere on the Paper to deselect the symbol. Press <F5> to refresh the screen if necessary.

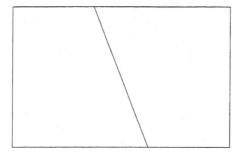

Two copies of Puzzle Piece A placed side by side

Place the First Triangle

The first of two triangles (Puzzle Piece B) must now be placed into position. No rotation is required.

1. The Select tool should still be active. If not, click on the Select tool in the Insert Entity toolbar.

2. Drag and drop a copy of Puzzle Piece B (from the symbol library palette) into the drawing, below the first two pieces.

3. Press the <Ctrl> key and move the selection cursor on to the reference point at the center of the symbol. When the cursor changes to the hand, click on the reference point.

4. Move the hand cursor to the upper left corner of the symbol, and click directly on the corner. The reference point will move to this new location.

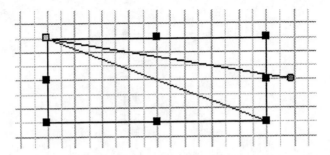

The reference point has been moved to the upper left corner of the triangle

5. Keep the cursor on the reference point, and it will change to the four-directional pointer. Drag and drop the reference point onto the lower left corner of the first symbol pair.

6. Click anywhere on the Paper to deselect the symbol. Press <F5> to refresh the screen if necessary.

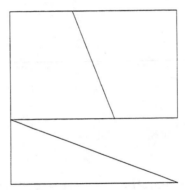

Three pieces of the square version of the puzzle are now in place

Complete the Square

One more triangle, and the square is completed. This fourth piece must be rotated 180 degrees, using the same rotation technique as before.

1. The Select tool should still be active. If not, click on the Select tool in the Insert Entity toolbar.

2. Drag and drop a copy of Puzzle Piece B (from the symbol library palette) into the drawing, to the right of the first three pieces.

3. Highlight "0" in the Rotation field of the Edit Bar. Type 180 and press <Enter>.

4. Press the <Ctrl> key and move the selection cursor on to the reference point at the center of the symbol. When the cursor changes to the hand, click on the reference point.

5. Move the hand cursor to the upper left corner of the triangle (which is also the upper left corner of the selection rectangle), and click directly on the corner. The reference point will move to this new location.

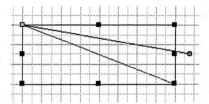

Move the reference point to the upper left corner of the triangle

6. Keep the cursor on the reference point, and it will change to the four-directional pointer. Drag and drop the reference point onto the same location used to place the first triangle—the lower left corner of the first symbol pair.

7. Click anywhere on the Paper to deselect the symbol. Press <F5> to refresh the screen if necessary. The square puzzle is completed.

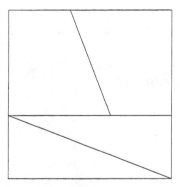

The completed square puzzle

Assemble the Rectangle Puzzle

Now comes the interesting part. When the four pieces are organized into a square, they cover 64 square inches. But when they are organized into a rectangle, they appear to cover 65 square inches. If you don't already know the reason behind this seemingly paradoxical situation, it will soon become visible.

If you took the time to create this puzzle from pieces of paper, you know that to form the rectangle you have to turn over the two triangles in addition to rotating them. Since it isn't possible to pick up and turn over the triangles in our drawing, we need another technique. The hard way would be to draw another symbol. A slightly easier way would be to Mirror

Copy the triangle (creating a mirror image), and erase the original. But the easiest way of all involves tricking TurboCAD into changing the *scale* of the triangle without changing the *size.*

Positive and Negative Scale

Normally the X Scale and Y Scale fields in the Edit Bar are used to change the size of an object. Scale values of less than one reduce the size of an object; scale values greater than one increase the size. A scale of .5 reduces an object to one-half its original size; a scale of 2 doubles the size of an object. To change the size of an object proportionally, both the X and Y scales must be changed equally.

By selecting a scale of negative one (-1) for either the X or Y dimension, the scale command can flip an object, using either a horizontal (X) or vertical (Y) axis.

To visualize how flipping an object with the scale command works, go back to the pencil on the desk. Lay the pencil horizontally. Hold the left end against the desk, and lift the right end up and flip it over, keeping the left end in position. This is the equivalent of setting the X (horizontal) scale to -1. Changing the orientation from positive to negative points the object in a reverse direction. Keeping the scale factor at 1 means the object maintains its original size.

To flip an object right to left, change the X scale to -1. To flip an object bottom to top, change the Y scale to -1. Both the X and Y scales can be changed to -1 if necessary.

Positive and Negative Rotation

The two copies of the four-sided polygon required to assemble the rectangle need to be rotated, not flipped. In the exercise above, objects were rotated 180 degrees, one-half the distance around a circle. It did not matter if the object rotated to the left or the right (counterclockwise or clockwise). But this time the required rotation is only 90 degrees, so the direction of rotation becomes important.

By default, rotation in TurboCAD is counterclockwise. To rotate an object clockwise, type a negative value for the rotation.

TIP: *In most CAD programs, positive numbers mean counterclockwise rotation, negative numbers mean clockwise rotation, and that is that. But it is possible in TurboCAD to change the positive direction of rotation, in effect swapping clockwise movement for counterclockwise. Use the Angle property of the Drawing Setup dialog (Menu: Tools|Angle) to make this change.*

Place the First Section of the Rectangle Puzzle

1. Use the scroll bars and move the symbol library palette if necessary to gain room to assemble the rectangle puzzle below the square.

2. Drag a copy of Puzzle Piece A onto the Paper, below the square puzzle.

3. Select the value in the Rotation Field (Edit Bar) and type -90 to rotate the selected symbol 90 degrees clockwise.

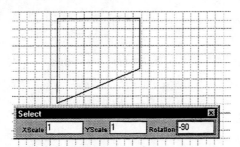

A value of -90 in the Rotation Field of the Edit Bar

4. Press the <Ctrl> key and move the cursor onto the reference point of the selection rectangle. When the cursor changes to a hand, click on the reference point.

5. Move the hand cursor to the lower left corner of the selection rectangle, and click directly on the corner. The reference point will move to this new location.

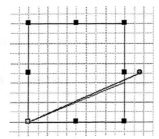

Reference point on lower left corner

6. Keep the cursor on the reference point, and it will change to the four-directional pointer. Drag and drop the reference point onto a grid intersection.

7. Click anywhere on the Paper to deselect the symbol. Press <F5> to refresh the screen if necessary.

Place the Second Section of the Rectangle Puzzle

1. Drag a copy of Puzzle Piece B (triangle) onto the Paper.

2. Select the value in the Y Scale Field (Edit Bar) and type -1 to flip the selected symbol vertically. The hypotenuse is now the bottom of the triangle, not the top.

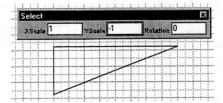

Using a value of -1 in the Y Scale field to flip the triangle

3.   Press the <Ctrl> key and move the cursor onto the reference point of the selection rectangle. When the cursor changes to a hand, click on the reference point.

4.   Move the hand cursor to the upper left corner of the selection rectangle, and click directly on the corner. The reference point will move to this new location.

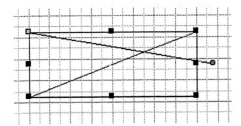

Reference point on upper left corner of triangle

5.   Keep the cursor on the reference point, and it will change to the four-directional pointer. Drag and drop the reference point onto the upper right corner of the previously placed (Piece A) object.

6.   Click anywhere on the Paper to deselect the symbol. Press <F5> to refresh the screen if necessary.

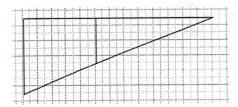

The first two pieces of the rectangle puzzle

Place Another Triangle

1.   Drag a copy of Puzzle Piece B (triangle) onto the Paper, below the last two objects placed.

2.   Select the value in the X Scale Field (Edit Bar) and type -1 to flip the selected symbol horizontally. The hypotenuse now faces to the upper left, not the upper right.

3. Press the <Ctrl> key and move the cursor onto the reference point of the selection rectangle. When the cursor changes to a hand, click on the reference point.

4. Move the hand cursor to the lower left corner of the selection rectangle, and click directly on the corner. The reference point will move to this new location.

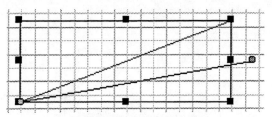

Reference point on lower left corner

5. Keep the cursor on the reference point, and it will change to the four-directional pointer. Drag and drop the reference point onto the lower left corner of the four-sided polygon.

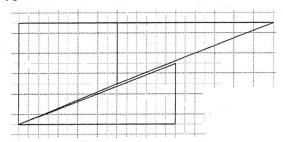

Correct placement for the latest triangle: notice the gap starting to form

6. Click anywhere on the Paper to deselect the symbol. Press <F5> to refresh the screen if necessary.

Place the Final Section of the Rectangle Puzzle

1. Drag a copy of Puzzle Piece A (polygon) onto the Paper.

2. Select the value in the Rotation Field (Edit Bar) and type 90 <Enter> to rotate the selected symbol counterclockwise.

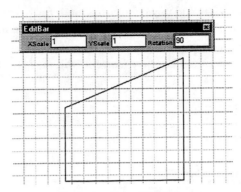

Rotate the polygon 90 degrees

3. Press the <Ctrl> key and move the cursor onto the reference point of the selection rectangle. When the cursor changes to a hand, click on the reference point.

4. Move the hand cursor to the upper right corner of the selection rectangle, and click directly on the corner. The reference point will move to this new location.

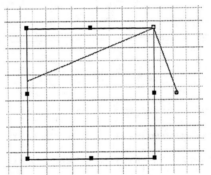

Reference point on upper right corner of polygon

5. Keep the cursor on the reference point, and it will change to the four-directional pointer. Drag and drop the reference point onto the upper right corner of the existing group of puzzle pieces. This will join the two corners at a grid intersection.

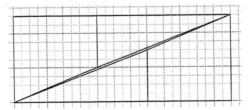

Correct placement for the final piece

6. Click anywhere on the Paper to deselect the symbol. Press <F5> to refresh the screen if necessary.

The Solution

Compare the square and the rectangle. Do you see the gap in the middle of the rectangle? You can measure that space, if you like. Use the multiline tool and Snap Vertex, and draw a line around the space. Use Local Menu|Close to finish. Then select the multiline and execute Menu: View|Selection Info. The area will be equal to 1. Multiplying the sides of the object to calculate square inches yielded 64 square inches for the square, because the adjoining sides of the objects meet at all points. But the same process yielded a product of 65 square inches for the rectangle, because the adjoining sides do not meet at all points, and an extra square inch is "trapped" inside.

Doing this exercise on paper isn't precise enough to notice the 1-square-inch gap. Using a paint-type program to sketch the problem would have been no better. But in CAD the solution is obvious.

Moving On

While you may never need to draw this geometric puzzle again, the techniques and commands used in this chapter are important ones. To review, this chapter covered: changing Paper scale and display; changing the on-screen view; window selection of objects; creating groups; creating and using symbols; rotating objects; flipping objects using negative scale references; and moving an object's reference point.

4
Keeping Design Simple

Draw, Trim, Mirror . . . Voila!

The adjective *simple* can be used in a derogatory sense, but most simple things hold great promise. Simple directions on how to drive to a friend's house will ensure success. Simple toys allow for greater imaginative input. Simple software products are more likely to be used than complex ones.

Simplicity in the realm of CAD means finding ways to create designs quickly and easily. The First Law of CAD (never draw the same thing twice), is a reflection of the need to keep things simple. The project in this chapter is a simple design. The techniques used to create it are simple. You only need to draw three circles and six lines. The Trim and Mirror commands make quick work of completing the design. By keeping things simple, it becomes possible to leapfrog quickly from a few lines to a complete project.

In this chapter you will draw a tape reel cartridge. There are three sections: the storage barrel, the exposure plate, and the take-up reel. Both the storage barrel and the take-up reel have gear teeth that fit over spindles. The storage barrel and the take-up reel are identical in size, giving the cartridge a symmetrical look.

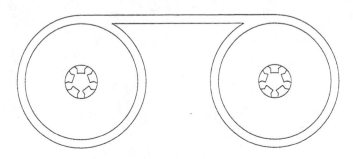

Project for this chapter: tape cartridge

The Design Environment

When starting a new project you need to start with two planning steps. The first is an evaluation of the design, to gain ideas on how to best draw your project. This evaluation leads to the second step, organizing TurboCAD to suit the requirements of the design.

TurboCAD offers a wide degree of flexibility in setting up the drawing environment. By *drawing environment,* we mean all the options and settings available in the program, as well as the *interface* (how the program presents itself to the user).

In the last chapter, attention was given to the settings related to groups and Paper space. This was an example of organizing the CAD program based on the needs of the project. In this chapter the Paper will again be adjusted, including the grid. The display of distances and coordinates will also be changed.

Most drawing environment settings are found in the Tools menu, in one of two dialogs. Program Setup and Drawing Setup were both used previously, and will be used again in this chapter. The drawing environment is not to be confused with *properties,* which refers to the characteristics of objects (to be covered in detail in Chapter Nine).

Start this project by adjusting the scale, the units, the grid, and the presentation of the Paper.

Adjust Drawing Settings

1. Launch TurboCAD and start a New drawing. Accept the Normal template.
2. Select Menu: Tools|Units and Scale dialog.
3. Under "Units in Work Space" change Format to Fractional, make sure Show All Units is checked, and set Precision to 4.

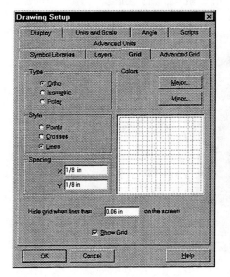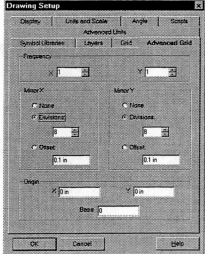

Grid and Advanced Grid dialogs, with settings as listed in the text

When fractions are used for coordinates and measurements, you must establish the level of precision. A Precision setting of 4 allows TurboCAD to identify distances as small as 1/16". A Precision setting of 8 would allow the program to display distances and locations down to 1/256"; a Precision setting of 2 would only display distances in 1/2" increments.

4. Click on the Grid tab.

5. Highlight the value for X Spacing and type 1/8 in.

6. Highlight the value for Y Spacing and type 1/8 in.

7. Make sure Show Grid is checked.

8. Click the Advanced Grid tab.

9. Under "Frequency" set both X and Y to 1.

10. Under both "Minor X" and "Minor Y," set Divisions to 8.

11. Click OK.

Spacing sets the distance between grid lines. *Divisions* sets how many minor grid spaces (not the lines that define the spaces) appear between each major line. By setting Spacing at 1/8" and Divisions at 8, the distance between each minor grid line (the lighter lines) will be 1/8" and the distance between each major grid line (the heavier lines) will be 1". Frequency determines how visible grid lines alternate with invisible grid lines. If Spacing were still 1/8" but frequency was 4, there would be invisible grid lines on the sheet. The Grid Snap command will snap to any grid point, visible or not.

Blue is the default color scheme of the grid. You can change the colors of both the major and minor grid lines using the Colors buttons in the Grid dialog. When you select either option, a color wheel appears. The scroll bar to the right of the color wheel controls relative color brightness. To change a color, click the desired shade on the color wheel.

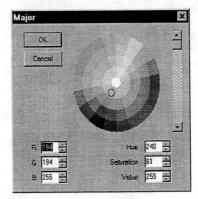

Major color wheel

12. Select Menu: Tools|Program Setup. Click on the Desktop tab.

13. In the Paper Display box, make sure both Show Margins and Show Background are checked.

14. Click OK.

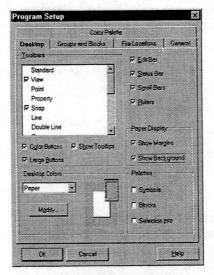

Desktop dialog in Program Settings

Draw Three Circles

Each side of the cartridge consists of three circles. These will be drawn using the grid and the Coordinate Display as references, to make sure they are the right size.

TurboCAD offers seven ways to make a circle, each available from a button in the flyout toolbar. The Ellipse tools are also on this flyout.

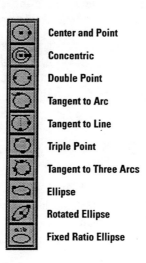

Center and Point

Concentric

Double Point

Tangent to Arc

Tangent to Line

Triple Point

Tangent to Three Arcs

Ellipse

Rotated Ellipse

Fixed Ratio Ellipse

Circle/Ellipse flyout toolbar

Here's how each tool works:

Tool	Action
Center and Point	Specify a center point and a radius
Concentric	Draw circles that share the same endpoint
Double Point	Define two opposite points to establish the diameter
Tan to Arc	Draw a circle tangent to an arc or another circle
Tan to Line	Draw a circle tangent to a line
Triple Point	Specify three points to establish the circumference
Tangent to 3 Arcs	Draw a circle tangent to three existing arcs or circles
Ellipse	Define a boundary rectangle to set width and height
Rotated Ellipse	Draw an ellipse rotated at any angle
Fixed Ratio Ellipse	Specify the ratio of the major axis length to the minor axis length

In this exercise only the Concentric circle tool will be used.

1. Select the Grid Snap tool and the Magnetic Point tool in the Snaps toolbar (left side of screen).

Grid Snap (left) and Magnetic Point

2. Select the Zoom Window tool in the Views toolbar.

3. Drag a selection window around the top left quarter of the paper. The screen will redraw with a close-up view of this area.

Zoom Window (left) and Concentric Circle

4. To start the first circle, select the Concentric Circle tool (as shown above). Click on the intersection of two major grid lines found at X 2" Y 6". Refer to the Coordinate Display at the bottom of the screen to help you find the right location.

5. Move the cursor up 1/4" (two grid lines) and click at X 2" Y 6 1/4" to finish the innermost circle as illustrated below.

6. Move the cursor up 5/8", to X 2" Y 6 7/8". Click to place a second circle.

7. Move the cursor up 1/8" (to the next major grid line), and click at X 2" Y 7". Right-click and choose Finish.

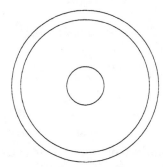

Three circles placed using the on-screen grid and the Concentric Circle tool

Draw Gear Tooth

In the finished drawing there are five gear teeth on each side of the cartridge. Each tooth is identical, so it is only necessary to draw one tooth; the others will be copied from the original.

The gear tooth will be drawn using a construction technique that takes advantage of the grid to simplify placement of the lines. A new snap, Middle Point, will also be used. When Middle Point is active, the exact midpoint of a line can be identified for use (to start or end a line, place a copy, etc.)

A rectangle will be drawn, but only part of it will remain in the drawing. Rectangles and other polygons are considered to be singular objects in TurboCAD, not a collection of individual lines. To remove pieces of the rectangle, it will have to be "exploded" first, or changed from a single entity to a collection of lines. The Menu: Format|Explode tool is used for this purpose. Parts of some lines will be trimmed off as excess before the tooth is finished, using the Menu: Modify|Object Trim tool.

This technique is only one of several approaches that could be used in TurboCAD to create the desired elements. We use this approach here so that you may experience the integrated use of drawing and editing tools.

1. Use Zoom Window to get a close-up view of the innermost circle.

2. Select the Line tool from the Insert Entity toolbar (top of screen).

3. Click on the grid at X 1 7/8" Y 6 1/4" to start a line. This location is one minor grid line left of a major grid line.

4. Move the cursor one grid line down and right, and click at X 2" Y 6 1/8".

First line of gear tooth intersects inner circle

5. Start the second line at the end of the first line (X 2" Y 6 1/8").

6. Move the cursor up and right to X 2 1/8" Y 6 1/4" to finish the line.

Second line drawn

7. Select Middle Point from the Snaps toolbar.

Middle Point Snap tool

8. Click and hold on the Line tool until the flyout toolbar appears. Select the Rectangle tool.

Rectangle tool

9. Click on the middle of the first line (the left line) at approximately X 1 15/16" Y 6 3/16".

10. Move the cursor down to the Coordinate Fields Display at the bottom of the screen (you can also press <Ctrl> <R>). Highlight the value in the X field. Type "2 1/16 in." and press <Tab>.

11. The value in the Y field is now highlighted. Type "6 1/8 in." and press <Enter>. A rectangle will be drawn.

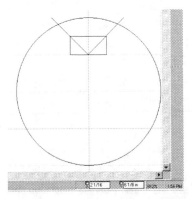

The Coordinate Display shows the correct values for finishing the rectangle

Explode Rectangle

1. Click on the Select tool.

2. Click on the rectangle. A selection rectangle will appear.

3. Select the Menu: Format|Explode command.

4. Click anywhere on the Paper to deselect the rectangle.

Trim and Delete Lines to Finish Tooth

This next section introduces the Object Trim command. It is used to cut off unwanted portions of lines or other objects. Object Trim cuts one object using an intersecting object as the cutting edge; the command does not allow you to cut away a portion of a solitary object. To use the command, you first identify the cutting edge. This is the overlapping object that will not be changed. Then you identify the object to be trimmed, clicking on the part of the line (arc, etc.) that will be trimmed away.

You may want to glance back at the finished design to help you understand how lines will be trimmed and deleted to finish the gear tooth.

1. From the menu, select Modify|Object Trim.
2. The prompt at the bottom of the screen reads "Define the cutting edge."
3. Click on the circle to identify it as the cutting edge. It will be highlighted.
4. The prompt reads "Add cutting edge (Shift) or select object to trim."
5. Click on the left angled line, *outside* the circle, to trim it away
6. Click on the right angled line, *outside* the circle, to trim it away.

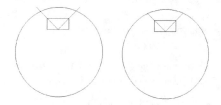

Before and after using Object Trim on the angled lines

7. Press <Esc> to deselect the circle as the cutting edge. The Object Trim command is still active, but you must now select a new cutting edge.
8. Click on the left side of the rectangle to select it as the cutting edge.
9. Press <Shift> and click on the right side of the rectangle. Now both sides are selected as cutting edges.
10. Click on the left angled line inside the rectangle.
11. Click on the right angled line inside the rectangle.
12. Click on the Select tool to end Object Trim.
13. Click on the top line of the rectangle. Press <Delete>.

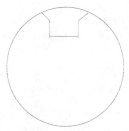

The lines inside the rectangle have been trimmed

Copy Tooth Around the Circle

The Fit Radial Copy tool will be used to make four new copies of the tooth, arrayed around the inside of the small circle. It is one of eight copy commands in TurboCAD. The Mirror command will be used later in this exercise; the others will be introduced later in the book.

Here's how each copy tool works:

Tool	Action
Linear Copy	Copy objects along a line (real or imagined) by stating the interval between each copy.
Radial Copy	Copy objects along an arc (real or imagined) by stating the angular spacing between each copy and the rotation of each copy relative to the previous copy.
Array Copy	Copy objects in a two-dimensional pattern by stating the vertical and horizontal spacing between objects.
Fit Linear Copy	Copy objects along a line by stating the total distance into which all the copies will fit.
Fit Radial Copy	Copy objects along an arc (real or imagined) by stating the total angular distance in which all the copies must fit and the rotation of each copy relative to the previous copy.
Fit Array Copy	Copy objects in a two-dimensional pattern by stating the dimension of the rectangle into which they must fit.
Mirror Copy	Create a mirror image of an object on the opposite side of a line that you specify.
Vector Copy	Make a single copy of an object, specifying both the angle and distance of the copy from the original

The difference between Radial Copy and Fit Radial Copy is that in Radial Copy you set the distance (in degrees) between objects; in Fit Radial Copy you specify the total angular distance (in degrees) for all objects, and TurboCAD will then determine the angular distance between each copy.

With either command, TurboCAD counts the original as one of the objects. So the number you want is actually the total number of objects required, not just the new copies required.

1. Choose the Select tool and then right click (Local Menu) to turn off Open Window mode. Only objects totally enclosed in a selection window will now be selected.

2. If necessary, use the Scroll Bars to adjust the view, so that the entire inner circle is visible. Draw a selection window around the five lines of the gear tooth. The lines will highlight and a selection rectangle will appear.

3. From the menu, select Edit|Copy Entities|Fit Radial.

4. A dotted-line circle appears on-screen. The prompt line reads "Define the center of the copy process."

5. Click on the grid intersection at the center of the circle (X 2" Y 6").

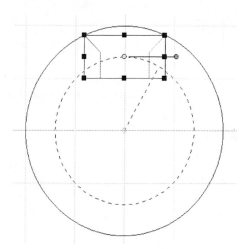

The rotation path and the angular distance appear as dotted lines when using the Fit Radial Copy command

6. The prompt reads "Define the angle to fit the copies in."

7. Move the cursor up to the Edit Bar. Highlight the value in Sets and type 6.

Currently, TurboCAD 3.0 has a defect — you must give a number one higher than the total number of Sets required in Fit Radial Copy. In this example, you must specify six sets to actually create the original and four new sets. The next release of TurboCAD will correct this problem.

8. Highlight the value in Angle and type 360.

Edit bar with sets and angle fields filled in

9. Press <Enter>. The tooth will be copied around the inside perimeter of the circle, for a total of five copies.

10. Click on the Select tool to end Fit Radial Copy.

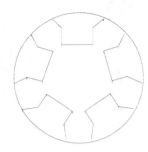

New copies of the gear tooth have been placed around the circle using Fit Radial Copy

Draw the Exposure Plate

Two parallel lines extending from the top of the outer circles represent the exposure plate. The Double Line tool will be used to draw the lines, then the Object Trim command will graft the lines into the take-up reel.

Double Line is actually one of eight tools that can draw parallel lines as a single entity. The eight tools are:

Tool	Action
Double Line Segment	Define two endpoints to draw a double line
Double Line Multiline	Draw a series of connected double lines
Double Line Polygon	Draw a double line polygon by providing the number of sides in the polygon and the distance from the center to one corner.
Dbl. Line Irregular Polygon	Draw a double line irregular polygon a side at a time.
Double Line Rectangle	Draw a horizontal double line rectangle.
Dbl. Line Rotated Rectangle	Draw a double line rotated rectangle to any angle.
Perpendicular Double Line	Draw a double line perpendicular to an existing line.
Parallel Double Line	Draw a double line parallel to an existing line.

Double lines have special properties, or characteristics, that you must choose before use. A double line dialog is available by right-clicking on a double line tool icon, or by selecting Menu: Format|Properties.

In the Double Line dialog you can:

- Set the distance between the two lines.

- Decide if the endpoints of the double line are to be open or closed (capped). Each endpoint can be set individually.

- Set the alignment of the double line. The options are left, right or center. If you choose left align, for example, the points you click on to identify the double line will become the left side. If you wanted a double line to straddle a series of points, you would choose Center Alignment.

To determine which is the left and which is the right side of a double line, imagine yourself standing on the starting point of the line, facing the endpoint. No matter which way you rotate the line, the right side remains on your right. This is similar to the terms "port" and "starboard" which define directions relative to the fore and aft of a ship. The critical thing is to know the direction in which the double line is drawn.

In the next sequence you will graft a double line to the outer circle. You will set the properties "on the fly" using the Local Menu (right click of the mouse on the double line tool). It is not necessary to explode the double line before using Object Trim to connect the line to the circle.

1. Click on Zoom Full View in the View toolbar.

Zoom full view

2. Click on Zoom Window in the View toolbar. Starting at the margin border in the upper left corner of the Paper, drag a selection window around the drawing that is six major grid squares wide and three major grid squares deep.

3. Click on Double Line in the Insert Entity toolbar.

Double line tool

4. Right-click on the Double Line tool to summon the Properties dialog. Click on the Double Line tab.

5. Highlight the value in the Separation field and type "1/8 in."

6. In the Reference section, click on the radio button for Left.

7. Click on OK.

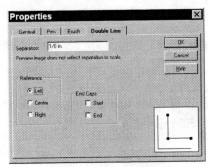

Double Line properties dialog

8. Move cursor to the top of the outermost circle. Click on the grid intersection at X 2" Y 7" to start the double line.

9. Move the cursor right 1 1/2" and click on the grid intersection at X 3 1/2" Y 7" to finish the line.

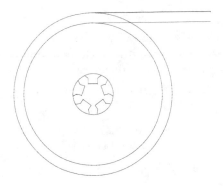

Double line drawn at top of circle

Graft Double Line to Circles

Use Object Trim to integrate the new double line into the top of the take-up reel.

1. From the menu, select Modify|Object Trim.

2. The prompt reads "Define the cutting edge." Click on the double line.

3. Click on the portion of the outer circle that passes between the double lines.

4. Press <Esc> to deselect the double lines as the cutting edge.

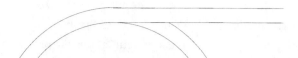

The portion of the outer circle in between the two double lines has been trimmed away

5. Object Trim is still active, awaiting selection of a new cutting edge. Click on the outer circle to select it as the cutting edge.

6. Click on the bottom double line *inside* the outer circle.

7. Click on the Select tool to end Object Trim.

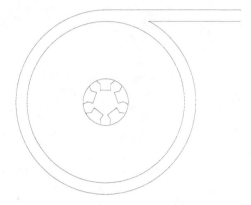

Trimming of double line and circles is completed

Mirror Copy to Finish Cartridge

One last step remains; to complete the object by creating a mirror image copy of the existing objects. Use the Mirror Copy tool whenever you need to create a mirror image of an object. The copy is placed using a line that you identify. If the line is a distance from the original, the copy will be the same distance away from the line on the opposite side.

Before you can mirror copy you will have to explode the double lines. If not, when you use Mirror Copy the new double lines will be mirrored both vertically and horizontally, giving an effect of flipping the double lines above the circle. (This happens because the double line is recorded as having a "left-to-right" orientation, which remains true after the Mirror Copy.) Try the sequence below without exploding first, if you like, to see this for yourself. Use the Undo tool to undo the wrong effect, and then explode the double lines before using Mirror Copy again.

1. Click on the double lines with the Select tool.

2. Select Menu: Format|Explode. The double lines are now two individual lines.

3. Draw a selection window around the entire drawing.
4. From the menu, select Edit|Copy Entities|Mirror.
5. The prompt reads "Define the first point of the mirror."
6. Click on the bottom right reference point on the selection rectangle.
7. The prompt reads "Define the second point of the mirror."
8. Click on the top right reference point uers the selection rectangle.

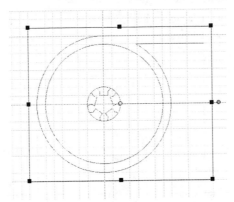

Use the reference points on the right side of the selection rectangle to set the location of the mirror edge

9. Click anywhere on the sheet to deselect objects and view the results of the mirror copy command.

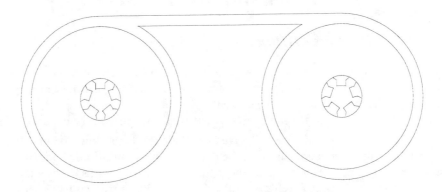

The completed cartridge

Looking for Design Technique Clues

It is quite common for experienced CAD users to integrate the use of drawing and editing commands to quickly create complex objects. There are clues to look for as you consider your project, clues that point to design shortcuts. Using the cartridge as an example, here are the design clues and the techniques suggested by each clue.

- The width of the tape path between reels, the width of the outer portion of each reel and the distance between the outer portion and the inner wheels are proportional. The grid spacing was set to match these proportions.

- The circles on each take-up reel have a common center, which means they are concentric. The use of the Concentric Center tool saved many keystrokes and mouse clicks when compared to the other circle tools.

- Drawing the first tooth at the top of the circle, centered on the (imagined) top-to-bottom diameter line, made it easier to visualize the symmetrical nature of each tooth.

- The combination of single lines, a rectangle, and Object Trim to draw the first tooth was one option; using Single Line Multiline was another. The line/rectangle/trim sequence required less step-by-step planning, because the intersection of the two single lines defined the bottom midpoint of the rectangle. In a reversal of an old cliche, in this situation function followed form.

- Once the first tooth was drawn correctly, Fit Radial Copy became the best tool for not only drawing the rest of the teeth, but for drawing the correct spacing between teeth without elaborate calculations. You could use Fit Radial Copy and the Undo tool to test various patterns, in effect using TurboCAD for initial design as well as drafting.

- The symmetrical nature of the completed cartridge suggests the use of Mirror Copy to save steps. An alternative method would have been to save the left side as a block, and then place the block using the flipping technique described in Chapter Three. But blocks are best used when there will be repeated placements of an object; in this drawing you would have only placed the block once. Plus, correctly placing the flipped block would be more complicated than using Mirror Copy on the original.

- Double Line was used to draw the exposure plate because of the way the bottom line intersected the outer circle (before it was trimmed). Trimming is the generally the easiest way to precisely connect a line to a circle when the line is not tangent or perpendicular. If Single Lines were used to draw the exposure plate, it would be been more complicated to draw the bottom line without using the Trim command.

Practice Makes Perfect

Try to practice the techniques presented in this chapter until they become routine. Object Trim, Explode, and the various copy commands are the most common non-drawing tools used in a CAD program. As you gain familiarity with them, they will become simple to use, and their usefulness will become obvious in a variety of situations.

5

The Designer View

The Power of Visual Feedback

Imagine yourself at a football game in a very large stadium. You have mid-field tickets, about 40 rows up. Good seats, great view, right? Now imagine there are no yard lines, no boundary lines anywhere on the field. From goal to goal, the field is solid green.

Kickoff time comes—where does the referee place the ball? If the kick goes into the end zone and is not returned, where is the 20-yard line? How will you know if a receiver runs out of bounds? If play is near the end zone, how can you tell if the ball is placed on the one-yard line or the four-yard line? Will the referees have to drag a measuring tape out for every play? Where would they measure from?

Fortunately, this is an imaginary game. Every real football stadium has yard markers and boundary lines on the field. These elements provide context known as *visual feedback*. Players, officials and fans can see what's going on, they can see where it happens, and they don't have to constantly measure and compute distances. As the game progresses up and down the field, a quick glance is enough to analyze and interpret all elements of the game related to field position.

TurboCAD provides visual feedback, too. You have already been introduced to three methods of visual feedback: the screen grid, the Paper, and the Coordinate Display. When the screen grid is active, you have an immediate sense of the size of objects. Using the grid as a guide, drawing objects on the screen is easier and more intuitive. Combine the visual feedback of an on-screen grid with the accuracy offered by Grid Snap, and you already have a drafting tool more useful than pencils and graph paper.

The grid and Grid Snap are only the beginning. TurboCAD provides visual feedback in other ways. This chapter will explore the various aspects of visual feedback in TurboCAD and how it relates to all other parts of the program. Concepts, tools and commands to be covered in this chapter include:

- Rubberbanding
- Snaps
- Magnetic Point
- Aperture

- Ortho
- The coordinate plane
- Absolute, Relative, and Polar coordinates
- Origin Point and Relocate Origin
- Zoom and Redraw

The screen elements common to all Windows programs are also part of visual feedback in TurboCAD. For help with such elements as scroll bars, menus, toolbars, selection arrows, etc., refer to your Windows documentation.

The features discussed in this chapter are found in the Modes menu and the View menu.

Rubberbanding

One of the most helpful visual feedback elements is called Rubberbanding. When you start to draw a line or any other geometric object, after you place the start of the object, the line (or circle, etc.) sticks to the cursor until you click to finish drawing the object. The ability to see a line or other object extend from the cursor makes it easier to see how the object will fit into the drawing. It may seem like a simple thing, but the lack of it would make drawing in TurboCAD much less intuitive.

Snaps

Snaps were briefly defined in Chapter Two, and have been mentioned several times since. A detailed discussion is now appropriate. Snap modes let you connect to exactly the kind of location you need. If you need to connect to the end (vertex) of a line, use Snap Vertex. If you need to connect to the midpoint of a line, use Snap Midpoint.

It is important to use snaps whenever possible for two reasons. The first is accuracy. Using snaps to connect lines and other objects allows you to take full advantage of the accuracy available in TurboCAD. Some new users, not realizing the importance of snaps, try to draw by "just coming close" when connecting lines. When the use dimensioning tools, they are surprised to find that objects in the drawing are not the exact sizes they should be.

The second reason to use snaps whenever possible is for efficiency. Snaps help you locate the point you need quickly. Consider the difference between finding the midpoint of a line by using Snap Midpoint, or by using a drafting construction technique. Using the snap, you immediately connect to the exact midpoint. Using the construction method, you must draw extra lines to find the exact same point.

You can define snap points that relate to objects, construction lines (covered in Chapter Six), and the grid. All snap mode functions are similar: You first set the snap mode, then click on or near the object that you want to snap to. Rather than placing the object exactly where you clicked the mouse, TurboCAD will place the object according to the snap mode in use. The exact location chosen depends on the snap mode in use. You can, for example, snap to the end of a line, the midpoint of a line, the center of a circle, or a point on the grid. Here is a list of snaps and their functions in TurboCAD:

Tool	Action
No Snap	Connection is made to the exact location of the mouse click. No Snap turns off any active snaps.
Snap to Vertex	Connect to the nearest end of a line segment, endpoint of an arc, or corner of a polygon, multiline or text element.
Snap to Nearest On Graphic	Connect to the nearest point on any entity.
Snap to Midpoint	Connect to the midpoint of a line segment.
Snap to Arc Center	Connect to the center of an arc or circle.
Snap to Quadrant Point	Connect to the nearest quadrant point (at 0, 90, 180, or 270 degrees) on the circumference of a circle or arc.
Snap to Intersection	Connect to the nearest intersection of two line segments.
Snap to Grid	Connect to the nearest grid point or intersection of grid lines.

Snaps and the Local Menu

You can change snap modes in three different ways. You can use the menu, the Snap toolbar, or the *local menu*. The local menu is available at any time while using TurboCAD by clicking the right mouse button. The local menu is context-sensitive: The specific commands and options available in the local menu change with the current activity. The concept of local menu is to provide you with suggestions of possible commands appropriate to the current activity. Not taking advantage of the local menu is like struggling to lift a heavy rock when a champion weight lifter has offered to do it for you. Timing is everything, and the programmers of TurboCAD have done a good job of choosing what commands and tools should be in the local menu at any given time.

When you choose a snap from the menu or the Snap toolbar, the effect is the same: The snap mode remains active until you reset it. The local menu is different. Use it for "one shot" mode changes, or *local snaps*. This means that when you change snap modes in the local menu, the snap you choose remains in effect only until you define the next point (finish drawing the object, etc.). TurboCAD then switches back to the last mode you set in the main menu or toolbar, or defaults to No Snap mode.

Local snap is useful because it lets you set the snap mode you use most frequently in the main menu or toolbar, then switch modes "on the fly" in the local menu as you draw. Many users like to set Grid Snap as their default snap mode, for example. But the need may arise to snap to a corner of a polygon not located on the grid. To do this, change the snap mode temporarily to Vertex (endpoint) in the local menu and define the point on the polygon corner. TurboCAD then automatically switches back to Grid Snap.

Combining Snap Modes

Some snap modes can be combined with one another, and some are mutually exclusive. No Snap turns off all other snap modes. Snap Nearest on Graphic (which snaps to the nearest point on any object) also turns off all other snap modes. Magnetic Point, defined later in this chapter (and used in the previous chapter), stays on no matter which snap modes are active.

The remaining snap modes all connect to a particular node (nodes are key points that define the object geometrically), and they are not mutually exclusive. For example, Snap to Grid and Snap Vertex can both be active at the same time. If both are on, and you click the mouse while a grid point and a line segment are both very close, the point will snap to either an endpoint of the line segment or to the grid point, whichever is closest to the mouse cursor. For a more detailed discussion of this kind of situation, see Aperture later in this chapter.

The snap modes that can be used at the same time are all in the same section of the Modes|Snaps submenu, and are displayed together in the Snaps toolbar. The No Snap tool will not turn off Ortho Mode (defined later in this chapter). Exercises throughout the rest of this book will introduce the various snaps not already used.

Magnetic Point

Magnetic Point visually identifies the location of snap points. The feature can be turned on or off. The menu location is Modes|Snaps|Show Magnetic Point. A check mark appears in the menu by the title when the feature is active. Its icon is located in the Snaps toolbar (left side of the screen).

Magnetic Point tool icon

When this Magnetic Point is active, as you move the mouse cursor within a critical distance from the snap point, the rubberband line will be attracted to the snap point, previewing its exact location. In other words, Magnetic Point scouts ahead to find potential connections that match the snap commands you have chosen. Unless you are using a slow computer, or unless you are working on a very large drawing, it is probably useful to have this mode on all the time.

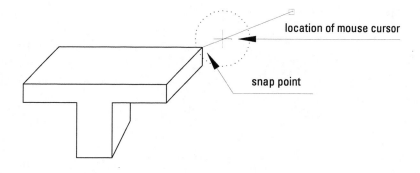

location of mouse cursor

snap point

Rubber band attracted to a snap point

Aperture

The phrase "a critical distance" was used in the last paragraph to describe how Magnetic Point assesses potential snaps. This critical distance between the point of the mouse click and the snap point is called the *snap aperture*. You can think of the snap aperture as a circle centered around the point of the mouse cursor. If a qualifying snap point is located within the snap aperture at the time of the mouse click, your action will connect to that snap point. If more than one object is located within the snap aperture, the connection will be made to the closest snap point.

To display the snap aperture, select Menu: View|Aperture. The aperture appears as a circle around the cursor. The radius of the snap aperture is controlled in the General property sheet of the Menu: Tools|Program Setup dialog.

TIP: *If you use the Coordinate Fields to define a point, you override any active snap.*

Ortho Mode

The word orthogonal comes from the Greek: "ortho-" means *straight and true;* "-gon" refers to object and angles. (Now if anyone ever says to you "CAD is all Greek to me" you can explain why.) Ortho mode in TurboCAD (Menu: Modes|Snaps|Ortho) limits the movement of the cursor if it is showing rubberband action as you create an object. By default, Ortho Mode will limit the angle of the rubberband to be parallel to either the X or Y axis. Another way to define this effect would be to say that an object can only be drawn to either true horizontal (a heading of either 90 or 270 degrees on the coordinate plane) or true vertical (a heading of either 0 or 180 degrees on the coordinate plane).

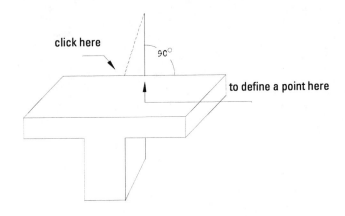

Drawing a line with Ortho mode active

Ortho mode can be modified to change both the specific headings (the direction a line points) and the number of degrees between headings. For example, you could force lines to be drawn at 30-degree increments starting at a heading of 10 degrees. The menu item to change the default Ortho setting is Menu: Tools|Drawing Setup|Angle.

The <Shift> key acts as a clutch to temporarily engage or disengage Ortho mode. If Ortho mode is on, and you need it off temporarily, use the <Shift> key to shut it off for the moment. Or, if Ortho mode is off, and you want it to help you draw just one line, press the <Shift> key as you draw the line.

The Coordinate Plane

The nature of the coordinate plane was introduced in Chapter One, but not explained in depth. The coordinate plane, and the various ways of using it, are fundamental to any CAD program. The objects you draw are stored in the drawing file by their location on the coordinate plane. TurboCAD offers three coordinate system modes: *Absolute, Relative,* and *Polar.* Absolute and Relative are based on the Cartesian coordinate system; Polar is considered as its own coordinate system.

Cartesian Coordinates

The Cartesian coordinate system starts with an origin point, through which two axes pass. The horizontal axis is X, the vertical axis is Y. You can name the location of any point on the coordinate plane by describing its distance along each axis from the origin. For example, to state the location of a point that is 2 units measured horizontally from the Y axis and 3 units measured vertically from the X axis, you would use the coordinates (2,3). For locations to the left of the Y axis or below the X axis you need to use negative values. To specify a location 2 units to the left of the Y axis and 2 units below the X axis, you would use the coordinates (-2,-2).

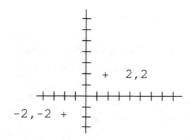

Points defined in Cartesian coordinates

Absolute Coordinates

The phrase *absolute coordinates* means you are defining the location of points on the coordinate plain relative to the origin point (0,0). The origin point never changes location unless you redefine it using the Page Setup dialog. By default, the origin is in the lower left corner of the page.

Relative Coordinates

Sometimes it is more important to know how far the cursor is from the last point placed than to know how far the cursor is from the origin point. The coordinate display can be adjusted to show that distance. This is known as *relative coordinates*. It means you are defining the location of points on the coordinate plain relative to the last point placed. If you are drawing with the Multiline tool, for example, every time you click to set another line, that particular endpoint becomes the new (0,0) location.

If the cursor is at (0,0), Absolute Coordinate Mode is active, and you move the cursor 1" up and 1" right, the coordinate display will show X 1" Y 1". If you start a line at this location and then move the cursor 1" up and 1" right again, the coordinate display will read X 2" Y 2". But consider the same actions if Relative Coordinate Mode is active. The cursor starts at (0,0) and moves X 1" Y 1". The *relative* coordinate display reads X 1" Y 1". But as soon as you click the mouse to define that point as the start of a line, the coordinate display reverts back to showing X 0, Y 0. Move the cursor another X 1" Y 1", and the coordinate display again reads X 1" Y 1", even though that's what it said a second ago. The difference is that you are now measuring the location of the cursor by its distance from the last point placed, rather than the origin point.

Another name used for relative coordinates in some CAD programs is Delta Coordinates, because the delta symbol (Δ) is the symbol for change in mathematics. When TurboCAD is displaying Relative coordinates, the plus-or-minus character ($\pm$) precedes the X or Y in the coordinate display.

An easy way to remember the difference between absolute and relative coordinate is to use the analogy of street addresses. If you say "my friend lives at 456 Mulberry Lane," you are saying a precise address, an *absolute* location. If you say "my friend lives three blocks from here," the description of your friend's home depends on where you stand when you say it: the description is *relative*. If you walk one block away and again say where your friend lives, relative to where you are standing, to be correct you would have to say four blocks instead of three. To give the absolute address, though, you would still say 456 Mulberry Lane.

For both absolute and relative coordinates, X is for left and right (horizontal) movement, and Y is for up and down (vertical) movement.

Polar Coordinates

The polar coordinate system takes the relative method of identifying locations and moves one step beyond. A polar location is defined by its distance and angle (measured from the horizontal) from the last point placed. As in the relative coordinate system, the relative origin follows the cursor as you work.

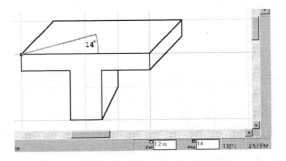

Points defined in polar coordinates

Drawing with Coordinate Systems

TurboCAD lets you change coordinate systems at any time while you are working. If you draw the outer wall of a house, for example, you may want to start the first wall at an absolute location in the drawing space, so you would use absolute coordinates for the first point. Each successive wall, however, would be defined by its length and angle relative to the first wall, so you might use polar coordinates for the remaining points.

Tɪᴘ: *Advanced users can "force" TurboCAD to use a coordinate system other than the current system when using the Coordinate Fields. If you precede a coordinate with the $ sign, it will be interpreted as an absolute coordinate; if you precede it with an @ sign it will be interpreted as a relative coordinate; if you precede it with a > sign it will be interpreted as a polar coordinate.*

Views of the Drawing Space

The TurboCAD drawing space is a plane on which you draw or place lines and other objects. A *view* is the area of the drawing space that appears on your screen. As your drawing becomes larger and more complex, it is important to be able to find views that let you work at the right location in the drawing, at an appropriate level of detail.

TurboCAD offers a variety of options for adjusting the view, known as panning (moving the view but not changing the resolution) and zooming (changing the resolution).

 TIP: *Another powerful way to control your view of the drawing is by selectively viewing layers, which will be introduced in Chapter Nine.*

Zooming

Zooming means to move in or out of the drawing space, viewing the drawing at a greater or lesser level of detail. The Zoom Window command was used in the last chapter; it is one of several zoom commands found in the menu at View|Zooms, or on the Zoom toolbar:

Command	Action
Zoom In	Move one step into the drawing.
Zoom Out	Move one step further from the drawing,
Zoom Window	Select a specific area to view.
View Extents	Zoom to a view that contains all of the objects in the drawing.
Full View	Display the full sheet.
Printed Size	View the drawing at the size it will be when printed.

An additional zoom command, Previous View, is not in the Zooms submenu, but is found at Menu: View|Previous View. This command is especially handy for switching back and forth between two views.

One quick and easy way to zoom is to use the plus and minus keys of the numeric keypad: plus zooms in one step; minus zooms out one step. The amount of each step depends on the *zoom factor,* which by default is 2. With the zoom factor at 2, Zoom In cuts the view in half, Zoom Out doubles the view. The zoom factor can be changed in the Menu: Tools|Program Setup dialog.

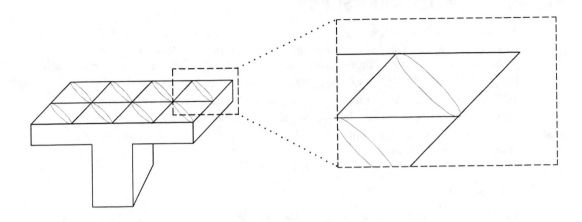

Zooming in on a view

When you zoom in and out using the plus and minus keys, the view centers on the mouse cursor. If you zoom in using a menu or toolbar command you will zoom in on the center of the current view, regardless of cursor location. As you zoom out, TurboCAD simplifies small objects to increase redraw speed.

 TIP: *To zoom in on a particular point in the drawing and place it at the center of the screen, place the mouse cursor over the point and press the <+> key on the numeric keypad.*

Panning

Panning means to move the view to another location across the drawing. TurboCAD provides two menu commands for panning, plus the scroll bars and the use of the arrow keys.

The scroll bars work the same way they do in other Windows programs. You can click the scrollbar arrow buttons to scroll one step, click in the body of the scrollbar to scroll about one-third of a screen, or drag the "thumb" of the scrollbar to move quickly across the drawing. The arrow keys are also simple and intuitive: press the up, down, left, or right arrow key to pan a single step.

 TIP: *To quickly pan to a specific point, place the mouse cursor at the point, then type <Ctrl> + <End>. The screen will instantly move to a view with the point you chose at the center of the screen.*

The Pan commands are found in the View menu:

Command	Action
Pan to Point	Scroll the drawing so that the point you choose is at the center of the screen.
Vector Pan	Choose a point and a destination and scroll the drawing so that the view moves to the destination.

Construction Technique: Divide the Area of a Triangle

The following tutorial will give you practice using some of the tools and commands covered in this chapter. The project is to divide the area of a triangle into five equal parts.

1. Launch TurboCAD, if not already running, and start a new drawing using the NORMMETR (Normal Metric) template.

2. Select the Zoom Window tool from the View toolbar along the right side of the TurboCAD desktop. Move the cursor to the upper left corner of the paper, and click to start a selection area. Move the cursor down and to the right until the selection rectangle covers the upper left quadrant of the paper, and click to zoom in.

Zoom Window tool icon

3. Select the Grid Snap tool from the Snaps toolbar along the left side of the desktop.

Grid Snap tool icon

4. Move the cursor to the Line tool on the Insert toolbar. Click and hold until the flyout toolbar appears. Select Irregular Polygon.

Irregular Polygon tool icon

5. Notice how the major grid lines form squares on the paper. To start the triangle, click once at the intersection of a horizontal major grid line and a vertical minor grid line.

6. To finish the left side of the triangle, move the cursor straight down to the next

horizontal major grid line, and click to set the line.

7. To draw the bottom line of the triangle, move the cursor three grid spaces to the right and one grid space up, and click to set the line.

8. To complete the triangle, right-click and select Finish from the local menu.

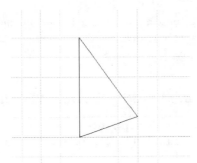

Triangle created using Irregular Polygon

9. Move the cursor into the center of the triangle. Press the plus key on the numeric keypad to get a close-up view of the triangle.

10. Select the Double Point Circle tool from the circle flyout toolbar.

Double Point tool icon

11. Click on each end of the first line (left line) of the triangle to draw a circle using the line as the diameter of the circle.

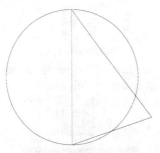

Add a circle to the triangle

12. Select the Single Line tool from the Line flyout toolbar.

Single Line tool icon

Next, using the horizontal minor grid lines as a guide, draw four lines perpendicular to the left side of the triangle.

13. To draw the first line, click on the line one grid intersection below the top. Move the cursor left so that the line will intersect the circle, and click on a grid point to end the line.

14. Repeat the process three times at the other intermediate grid points along the left side of the triangle. These lines divide the left side of the triangle into five equal parts.

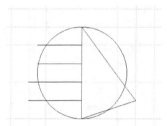

Draw four perpendicular lines that intersect the circle on the left

15. Select the Concentric Arc tool from the Arc flyout toolbar of the Insert Entity toolbar.

Concentric Arc tool icon

16. Select the Snap Intersection and Magnetic Point tools from the Snaps toolbar (along the left side of the TurboCAD desktop).

Snap Intersection (left) and Magnetic Point tool icons

Next draw a series of arcs intersecting the left side of the triangle. Each arc will start at the intersection of the dividing lines and use the top corner of the triangle as the center.

17. For the first arc, start by clicking at the top corner of the triangle, to set the center of the arc.

18. Click on the intersection of the top dividing line and the circle, to set the radius.

19. Click again at this same location to set the start of the arc.

20. Move the cursor to the right and click on a grid point that allows the arc to pass through the left side of the triangle.

21. The Concentric tool remains active, and has identified the center of the first arc for use again.

22. Move the cursor to the intersection of the second dividing line and the circle, and click to set the radius.

23. Click again at this same location to set the start of the arc. Move the cursor to the right and click on a grid point that allows the arc to pass through the left side of the triangle.

24. Repeat the steps above to draw two more arcs, to match the illustration.

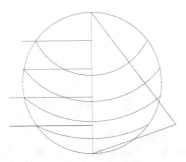

Draw concentric arcs that intersect the left side of the triangle

25. Select the Parallel Line tool from the Single Line flyout toolbar of the Insert Entity toolbar.

Parallel Line tool icon

26. The Parallel Line tool draws a straight line parallel to a line you select. Click on the bottom line of the rectangle. To draw a line parallel to it, click on the nearest intersection of an arc with the left side of the triangle. Continue the process, drawing lines that are parallel to the bottom line of the rectangle and have the intersection of the left side and an arc as one vertex. The regions defined inside the triangle by the parallel lines are equal in area.

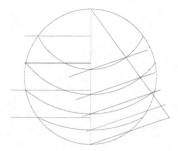

Parallel lines define equal areas of the triangle

27. Click on the Select tool in the Insert Entity toolbar.

28. Press and hold the <Shift> key, then click on every object in the drawing except the triangle and the intersecting lines that defines the equal areas. Press the <Delete> key to delete these objects.

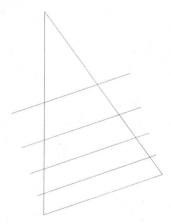

Delete unnecessary lines

29. Save the completed drawing in the IMSI/TCW30/Drawings subdirectory (or folder, in Windows 95) as DIV-TRI (if using Windows 3.1) or Divided Triangle (if using Windows 95). This drawing will be used in another exercise later in the book.

A Better View of the Action

Not all the features mentioned in this chapter were used in the tutorial. You may need to refer back to the explanations in this chapter as the other commands are used. Practice zooming and panning, using various snaps, and explore differences between relative, absolute and polar coordinates as you draw. Experiment and see if you develop preferences for any of the many kinds of visual feedback available in TurboCAD.

6

Introduction to Drawing Techniques

Lines and Angles

This is the first of two chapters devoted to a set of drawing techniques known as *geometric construction*. Don't let the phrase intimidate you; it only means taking advantage of geometric objects and their relationships. This chapter will cover the use of straight lines, polygons and angles, Chapter Ten will cover the use of circles, arcs, ellipses and curves.

Practicing these techniques will accomplish two goals. One, you will become more familiar with the capabilities of TurboCAD; and second, you will learn techniques that can be applied to a variety of drafting situations, no matter how you intend to use TurboCAD.

Basic Definitions

If too many years have passed since high school geometry, a quick review is in order. These are the common terms to be familiar with:

Point. A point is an exact location on a drawing surface. TurboCAD offers a Point tool, for marking these locations with one of five marks. The four geometric shapes (Star, Square, Cross, and Circle) can be adjusted for size; Dot cannot. Right-click on the Point tool, then select the Point tab, to access the Size setting.

TurboCAD offers five point styles, including a tiny dot (enlarged at left)

Line. A line is the measured distance between two points. A straight line is the shortest distance between two points. Generally in this book when it says "line" it means straight line.

Angle. An angle is the shape made by two straight lines meeting at a point. Angles are measured in degrees. One degree is 1/360 of the distance around a circle.

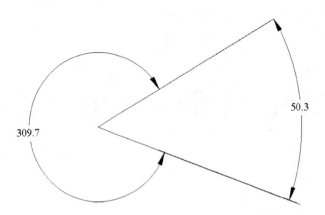

The angle formed by the meeting of two lines can be measured from both the inside and the outside

Circle: A circle is a closed curved line with all points on the line the same distance from the center point. A circle has three parts:

- *Diameter,* the straight distance from one point on the circle through the center to the opposite side.
- *Radius,* the straight distance from the center point to the outside line.
- *Circumference,* the length of the line around the center point.

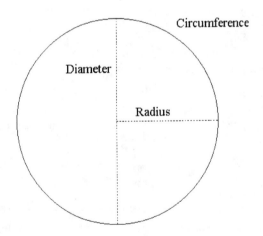

Parts of a circle

Arc. A portion of the circumference of a circle.

Ellipse. A closed curved surface that looks like a stretched circle. An ellipse is a precisely constructed object, defined as the path of a moving point so that the sum of its distances from two fixed points is constant. The Greek root of the word ellipse means "to fall short."

Literally, the Greeks considered an ellipse to be an attempt at a circle that fell short.

Tangent. A line that comes into contact with another, yet the two lines do not intersect if extended. In general use, arcs and circles are drawn tangent to straight lines (and vice versa) or to other arcs and circles.

Chord. A chord is a straight line that connects the two endpoints of an arc.

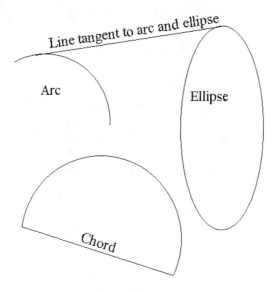

An arc, an ellipse, a tangent line, and a chord

Parallel. When two straight lines do not intersect, and remain the same distance apart at all points along the length, they are parallel.

Perpendicular. When one straight line meets another at a 90-degree angle (also known as a right angle), they are perpendicular. If one line is at true vertical, a line perpendicular to it is at true horizontal.

Bisect. To bisect is to divide something into two equal sections. In this chapter you will bisect lines and angles.

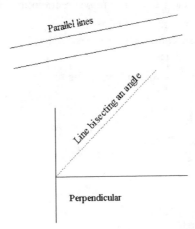

Parallel lines, perpendicular lines, and a line bisecting an angle

Polygon. A polygon is an object with three or more straight sides that form a closed figure. A regular polygon is a polygon with all sides the same length.

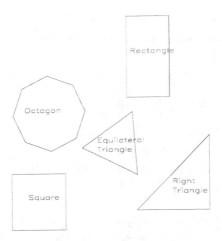

A variety of polygons

Triangle. A triangle is a three-sided polygon. It has three straight lines and three interior angles. An equilateral triangle is one with each side of equal length.

Rectangle. A rectangle is a four-sided polygon in which all angles are right angles and opposite sides are parallel.

Square. A square is a four-sided polygon in which all angles are right angles and all sides are the same length. By definition, a square is also a rectangle.

Measuring Distances, Angles and Areas

Sometimes as you draw you will need to know the exact length of a line, or at what angle two lines meet, yet it isn't necessary to dimension the object. The Menu: View|Selection Info command provides access to the information you need. To use the command, select an object, then select the command from the View menu. The Selection Info palette will appear, with information on the selected object.

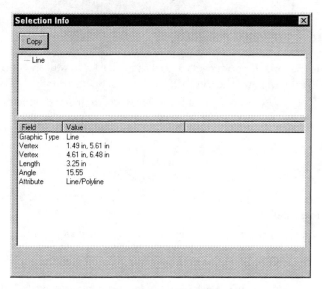

The Selection Info palette display for a line

In the above illustration, the Selection Info palette displays information on a line. The X,Y locations of each endpoint are listed (Vertex), then the length, the angle (or heading) of the line, and the object's attribute status (classification) in TurboCAD.

The Selection Info palette contains two windows. The upper window shows the type and structure of the objects selected. If a group, symbol or block is selected, the relationship of the items inside the object will be shown in outline form. A plus sign next to a item indicates that it contains other items that are not displayed. To open the outline, and see what objects are contained, click on the plus sign; click again to close the outline to see a higher level of the hierarchy.

The lower window displays precise data about whatever object is currently selected in the upper window. It shows the object's graphic type, its coordinate location in the drawing space, and its dimensions in current World units.

Pressing the Copy button copies this data to the Windows clipboard so that you can paste it into a word processor or text editor, such as Windows Notepad. The text that you copy contains special markers so that programmers, or adventurous users, can "parse" the data into their own programs.

NOTE: *Experienced users of the World Wide Web may notice that the markers are similar to those used in HTML, HyperText Markup Language.*

When straight lines are drawn in TurboCAD, they point in a specific direction, called a heading. This heading is listed as the angle in the Selection Info palette. The angle listed is the direction the line points away from the 0,0 origin point of the drawing. A line drawn at true horizontal can be listed in the Selection Info palette as having either an angle of 0 degrees or 180 degrees. Follow the exercise below to test this for yourself.

Draw Lines and Compare Angles

1. Start TurboCAD, if you haven't already, and start a new drawing (File|New). Select the normal template, and click OK to exit the Setup Dialog.

2. Click on the Snap to Grid tool from the Snaps toolbar, left side of the screen.

Snap to Grid tool

3. Draw a short line from left to right that starts at a major grid line and ends two major grid lines later.

4. Draw a second short line exactly the same distance as the first, but draw it from right to left.

5. From the menu, select View|Selection Info.

6. Click on the Select tool, and draw a selection window around both lines. An outline tree appears in the upper Selection Info window, "Line-Line."

7. Click on the first "Line" listed. The data for the top line on-screen appears in the bottom window.

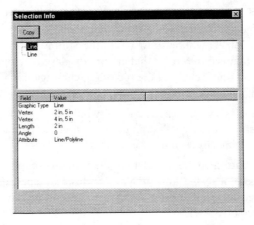

Selection info palette with data on two lines; first line's data appears in bottom half of dialog

8. Note the angle listed.
9. Click on the second "Line" listed in the outline. The data for the bottom line on-screen appears in the bottom window of the Selection Info palette. Again, note the angle listed.

If you are confused by how TurboCAD determines the heading of a line, picture that each line you draw starts from the 0,0 origin. If you go straight right, you are drawing a line with a zero-degree heading (angle). If you draw straight left, you are drawing a line with a 180-degree angle. Drawing a line from left to right at what looks like a 45-degree angle would be interpreted by TurboCAD as a 45-degree angle. But if you draw the same line from right to left, it may look like it sits at a 45-degree angle, but to TurboCAD it sits at 225 degrees.

Compute the Angle of Two Lines

TurboCAD does not provide a specific command for measuring the angular distance between two lines, as some CAD programs do. But such a command really isn't necessary in TurboCAD. It is so easy to use the Angular Dimension command, and then to erase the dimension if not needed, that a separate "measure angle" command would be redundant. Dimensioning commands are covered in detail in Chapter Eleven.

Measure the Area and Perimeter of a Polygon

You may use the Selection Info palette to measure both the area and the perimeter of a polygon created using a polygon tool or a multiline tool. The current World units will be the unit of measurement. If a polygon is created by drawing single lines that connect, the Selection Info palette will not recognize them as a polygon. This is true even if you use the Group command on the lines. If you know that you will need to know the area of an object in the drawing, be sure to draw it with a polygon (or trace over it on an unused layer with a multiline).

Construction Techniques

The rest of this chapter covers a variety of construction techniques using lines, angles and polygons. Chapter Ten will cover arcs, circles, ellipses, curved objects and their relationships to other objects. As you move from one example to the next, think about how you can take advantage of these techniques in your own design and drafting work. A few new commands will be presented along the way.

These construction techniques are presented in a generic fashion, so that you can use the steps in a real drafting setting as required. To practice them now, start each technique by drawing the required line or lines.

If you were to enroll in a traditional drafting course using pencil and paper, you would study the concepts presented below, but the methods used would be much different. The first technique is a good example of the tremendous difference between manual drafting techniques and automated drafting using a program like TurboCAD.

Bisect a Line with a Point

The first geometric construction technique taught in a manual drafting class is how to bisect a line. Using manual methods, bisecting a line requires the use of a straightedge and a compass. Two arcs and a second line must be drawn to correctly bisect the line. The process takes several steps. The technique is much easier in TurboCAD:

1. Given any straight line, select Middle Point from the Snap toolbar (left side of screen). All other Snap tools should be off.

2. Click on any point along the line. TurboCAD will calculate the exact center of the point, bisecting it for you. You may optionally select Middle Point Snap as a local snap (active one time only) with a right-click when you need it.

If you need to draw from the bisection point, the Line tool should be active before you select Middle Point Snap. If you need to mark the location, select a point mark from the Point tool on the Select Entity toolbar before selecting Middle Point.

A straight line marked with a point

Bisect a Line with a Perpendicular Line

1. Given a single line at any angle, start by making sure all Snaps are off. Click the No Snap button in the Snaps toolbar.

No Snap tool icon

2. Select Parallel Line from the Single Line flyout toolbar.

Parallel tool icon

3. Click on the existing line. Press <Tab> twice and type a number to set the distance between the two parallel lines. End by pressing <Enter>. This distance will become the length of your perpendicular line. One-half-inch (.5) was used in the illustration.

Draw a line parallel to the existing line

4. Click and hold on the Parallel Line tool icon, until the flyout toolbar appears. Select Single Line.

5. Select Middle Point Snap from the Snaps toolbar.

Middle point snap tool

6. Click on each line. A new line will connect the midpoints of each parallel line. This new line is perpendicular to the original line.

7. Delete the extra parallel line.

Draw a Line at a Specific Heading

1. Select the Line tool.

2. Start the line where required, using any snap tool if needed.

3. Type the length of the line in the Length field on the Edit Bar. Press <Tab> to select the highlighted field in the Edit Bar or simply type and the figures will appear in the highlighted field.

Edit bar, showing Length and Angle of a line

4. Press <Tab> to select the Angle field of the Edit Bar. Type the angle (the required heading of the line) and press <Enter>.

NOTE: *It does not matter whether TurboCAD is in Absolute, Relative or Polar mode. The Edit Bar will display Length and Angle when the Line tool is selected.*

Bisect an Angle

To bisect an angle is to divide an angle equally with a third line. Given any two lines that meet at a common endpoint to form an angle, use Fit Radial Copy to draw a line that bisects the angle. This method creates an extra line that must be deleted when the angle has been bisected.

The line to select for the Fit Radial Copy is the one that must be copied counterclockwise toward the other line. Depending on the orientation of the lines and the angle to bisect, the line to copy might be above or below, left or right, of the second line. Use the illustrations as a guide to see how the procedure works.

1. Draw two lines as illustrated below. Use No Snap or Grid Snap to draw the first line; use Vertex Snap (with all other snaps off) to draw the second.

2. Click on the Select tool.

3. Make sure Vertex is the only active snap.

4. Select the line that is on the clockwise side of the angle.

5. From the menu, select Edit|Copy Entities|Fit Radial.

6. The prompt reads "Define the center of the copy process." Click on the common endpoint of the two lines.

7. In the Edit Box, select the value for Sets and type 3.

8. The prompt reads "Define the angle to fit the copies in." Click on the distant endpoint of the second line.

9. A new line appears between the first two, which bisects the angle. An extra line has also been created; it is on top of the second line (the line not copied). Select it and press <Delete>.

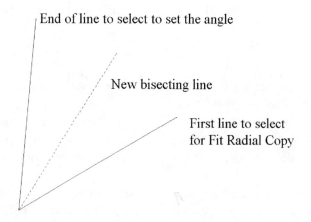

End of line to select to set the angle

New bisecting line

First line to select
for Fit Radial Copy

Bisecting an angle with a line

Divide an Angle Into Any Number of Parts

With only one change, the steps above used to bisect an angle can also be used to divide an angle into any number of equal parts. Instead of typing 3 in the Sets field of the Edit Bar, type a number that is one higher than the number of ways you need to divide the angle. Remember to delete the extra line on top of the line which was not copied.

Draw a Line Parallel to an Existing Line

TurboCAD has a double line command, which you can use when you need to draw two parallel lines. But when you need to create a line that is parallel to an existing line, use the Parallel Line tool, as described in Chapter Five, and as used in the technique above to assist in drawing a perpendicular bisecting line.

Divide a Straight Line into Proportional Parts

Two methods are available to divide a straight line into proportional parts. The first technique does not "break" the line into separate pieces, but marks off equal distances along the line, just as you would on paper with a pencil and a ruler. This technique uses the Menu: Edit|Copy Entities|Linear command to copy a Point marker along the distance of the line. Once the points are placed along the line, they can be snapped to with the Vertex Snap tool.

The second technique to divide a straight line into proportional parts used Node Edit, and is discussed in detail below.

Divide a Straight Line into Proportional Parts using Linear Copy

1. Draw a line, using any construction method of snap you prefer.

2. Click the No Snap tool.

3. Press and hold on the Point tool until the flyout toolbar appears. Select the Star shape (or any other shape you prefer).

4. Click Vertex Snap. Click on one endpoint of the line to place a star.

5. Use the Select tool to draw a closed selection window around the star. (To close the selection window right-click to get the local menu and turn off Open Window mode.)

6. From the menu select Edit|Copy Entities|Fit Linear.

7. The prompt reads "Select the final position of the reference point."

8. Press the <Tab> key until Sets is highlighted in the Edit Bar. Type a value that is one higher than the number of line segments you need to identify.

9. Click on the opposite end of the line to shift activity back to the drawing screen, and again to select the end of the line for the copy command. The stars will copy along the line.

Divide a Straight Line into Proportional Parts using Node Edit

Nodes are hidden markers that identify elements of geometric objects in TurboCAD. A straight line, for example, has two nodes, one at each end. A triangle drawn using Irregular Polygon has three nodes, one at each corner.

In Node Edit mode you can reshape entities by directly manipulating nodes. Appendix B of the TurboCAD 3 for Windows User Manual lists detailed instructions for using Node Edit for a wide variety of tasks. One of the available options in Node Edit is to divide line segments into any number of subsegments of equal length.

1. Draw a line, using any construction method of snap you prefer.

2. Select the line.

3. Right-click to summon the Local Menu. Select Node Edit.

The appearance of the selection changes when you shift to Node Edit mode. Instead of a selection box with handles, you will see hightlighted objects with nodes displayed as blue rectangles.

4. Place the mouse cursor on the line.

5. Right-click to open the Local Menu and choose Segment Divide. The Divide Segment By dialog appears.

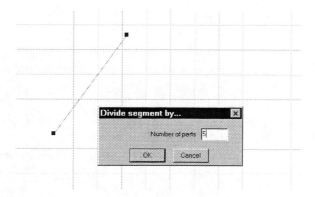

Divide Segment By dialog

6. Enter the number of parts into which you want to divide the line, then press <Enter>.

7. Click anywhere on the Paper to deselect the line.

The line looks no different unless selected for Node Edit. But now the line has nodes that divide it into proportional segments. You can snap to any of these nodes with Snap Vertex — they do not need to be visible.

Draw the Golden Mean of a Line

The golden mean is a length that represents the golden ratio, a distance used by ancient philosophers and modern designers. The relationship between a line and its golden mean (as in drawing the sides of a rectangle or right triangle) is universally appreciated as aesthetically pleasing. Given any line, the golden mean of that line has a ratio of .618 to 1. For example, if a given line is 1 unit in length, that line's golden mean will be .618 units in length.

To draw the golden mean of a line in manual drafting, it is necessary to place three arcs and an extra line. But in TurboCAD it is much easier. If you know the length of the original line, use the Windows Calculator (or pencil and paper) to multiply the length by .618. The product is the length of the line's golden mean. Use the Edit Bar to set the length of the new line.

Follow the steps below to draw a right triangle; the height will be the golden mean of the base. The distance of the base line in this example will be 3.65 inches. You can also use this procedure to draw a rectangle of golden mean proportions.

1. Select Irregular Polygon from the Line flyout toolbar, and Ortho Mode from the Snaps tool bar.

Irregular Polygon tool icon (left) and Ortho Mode tool icon

2. Click on the drawing sheet to start the triangle. Move the cursor to the right, then press <Tab> to switch to the Edit Bar. Type 3.65 <Enter> to set the length of the baseline.

3. Move the cursor up, then press <Tab>. Type 2.557 (the product of 3.65 times .618) and press <Enter> to set the height of the triangle.

4. Right-click and select Finish from the Local Menu. TurboCAD will close the triangle.

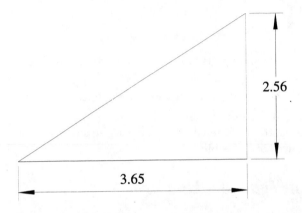

The ratio of the height to the base is the ratio of the golden mean (.618:1)

Construction Lines and Circles

As you draw, there may be times when you would like to use a line or circle for visual reference, but don't want to add a new entity to the drawing. Use a construction line or circle for this purpose. From the menu, select Insert|Construction and select one of six choices : Horizontal, Vertical, Angular, Center and Point Circle, Double Point Circle, and Triple Point Circle. If you select a line, it will cross the entire desktop. Construction circles are drawn to the size you specify.

You can place construction lines and circles with snaps, and can snap to them with any relevant snap command.

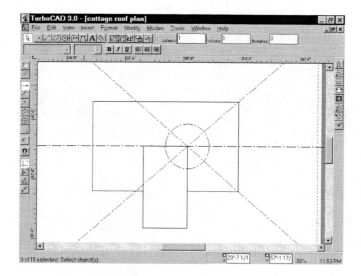

Construction lines appear as dot-dash lines in a drawing

Construction lines exist on their own layer, called $CONSTRUCTION. You can edit their appearance (line type and color) by editing the $CONSTRUCTION layer (Menu: Tools|Layer). Construction lines are for visual reference only, and cannot be selected like an entity or an object (with the exception of Nearest Entity Snap). Use the options at Menu: Edit|Clear to delete construction lines.

Aligning Objects

To create drawings in TurboCAD is to move back and forth between phases of drawing (when you create) and editing (when you modify). At times, you might realize that some objects in the drawing need to be rearranged so that they are aligned to each other. TurboCAD offers seven align commands for this purpose, found in the Format menu.

To use any of these commands, select the objects you wish to align:

Align Bottom will move the selected objects to the bottom of the selection's bounding box.

Align Along Line will move the selected objects along a construction line that you place.

Align Middle will center the selected objects vertically in the selection's bounding box.

Middle alignment, before (left) and after

7
Editing the CAD Drawing

Freedom to Create a Perfect Design

As you begin to draw with TurboCAD, you will find the ease and speed of drawing encourages you to make changes as you go along. Instead of using a rubber eraser, you can use TurboCAD's editing and modification commands to quickly rearrange, reshape, copy, replace or otherwise alter any part of a drawing.

The ability to make changes quickly and easily is part of what makes a CAD program superior to manual drafting. The experienced manual draftsman can quickly put lines on paper. But when it comes to making changes, the manual draftsman is left in the eraser dust by the power and versatility of a good CAD program.

The freedom to make changes is part of what makes TurboCAD a tool for both design (the creative process of deciding features) and drafting (the graphic representation of a design).

Edit or Modify?

Generally speaking, the phrase used to describe making changes to a CAD drawing is *editing*. But the commands in TurboCAD for making changes have been organized in two categories: Editing and Modifying. There is a menu for each, the Edit menu and the Modify menu, as well as a toolbar. For our purposes here, the following definitions apply.

Editing is *manipulation of existing objects*. If you need to copy an entity, remove it, move it, or place it in a file created by another program, you are editing. Many editing commands make use of the Windows clipboard. Under this definition, editing usually means the original entity is not reshaped, but there are exceptions, to be covered in this chapter.

Modifying is *alteration of existing entities*. If you need to cut a line, join two lines, or otherwise change the shape of one or more entities, you are modifying.

There are two practical differences between the tools in the Modify menu and the Edit menu. The first difference involves selection. When you use the Edit menu tools, you must first select the object or objects that you want to edit. Then you execute the operation on the selected object or entity (move, copy, erase, etc.) The Modify menu tools are similar to drawing tools, in that you first activate the tool, and then follow a series of steps to complete the edit. The operation is performed on entities that have not been previously selected. When you finish the operation, the tool remains active so that you can modify another object. You must switch to another tool to shut off the first tool.

The second distinction concerns the difference between *objects* and *entities*. As you will remember from Chapter Two, *object* is a general term that means anything that can be displayed in a TurboCAD drawing. This covers not only classical geometric primitives like lines, circles and curves, but also text and bit-mapped images. Objects can be groups of entities, or other elements of a drawing not easily defined using geometric definitions. The term *entity* is more specific. It means a drawing element created with TurboCAD drawing tools. Entities include single lines, multilines, arcs, circles, polygons, and so forth, as well as construction lines and circles. Entities are independent geometric elements. They would be at home in a geometry textbook, or a manual drafting course.

Editing tools work on both objects and entities. Modifying tools work only on entities. In practice, you use the tool or command that gets the job done, no matter its category. Knowing the difference between editing and modifying is largely a matter of gaining familiarity with the available tools.

Modify the Divided Triangle

The rest of this chapter is given over to tutorials that explore the use of various editing and modifying commands. The first exercise will be to make changes to the triangle drawn in Chapter Five, which was divided into sections of equal area. When the exercise was completed, the lines which divided the triangle had not been trimmed. You will do so now.

If you have not completed the exercise in Chapter Five, or did not save it, you can quickly draw a triangle and then draw some single lines over the top of it, to create an approximate version of the object described below. While the new version won't be divided into areas of equal size, you can still trim the lines as explained below.

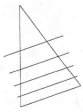

Divided triangle from Chapter Five

1. Launch TurboCAD. When the Create from Template dialog appears, click the Open

button. This allows you to open an existing drawing. In Chapter Five, you were directed to save the drawing in the IMSI/TCW30/Drawings subdirectory (or folder, in Windows 95) as DIV-TRI (if using Windows 3.1) or Divided Triangle (if using Windows 95). Open the drawing from this subdirectory/folder, or from wherever you saved it.

2. Select Object Trim from the Modify menu. (Object Trim was introduced in Chapter Four.)

3. The prompt at the bottom of the screen reads "Define the cutting edge."

4. Click on the triangle, which will change color (highlight) to show that it is selected.

5. One by one, click on each section of line *outside* the triangle. Each line will be trimmed to the triangle as you go.

6. Click on the select tool to end the command.

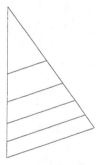

All intersecting lines have been trimmed to the edges of the triangle

Seeking Out the Details

To explore some of the editing and modifying tools, open a drawing that shipped with your copy of TurboCAD called WDET.TCW, an excellent wall detail drawing.

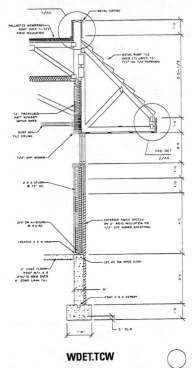

WDET.TCW

Notice that two portions of the drawing are circled. The circles identify portions of the drawing that were to be available separately as details. Follow the steps below to separate the circled elements from the rest of the drawing.

Before making any changes to WDET, the first item of business will be to save a second version of the drawing, so that the original is left intact.

1. Start TurboCAD, and open the drawing WDET.TCW, in the IMSI/TCD3/Samples directory (Windows 3.1 or NT) or folder (Windows 95).

2. From the menu, select File|Save As. In File Name, type CH7WDET. Change directories, selecting the IMSI/TCD3/Drawings directory (Windows 3.1 or NT) or folder (Windows 95). Click on the Save button, and fill in the details in the Summary Info dialog if you desire. Click on the OK button to end. The name of the file as listed in the Title Bar will change to CH7WDET.

Explode Groups, Extract Details

1. The entire WDET drawing has been gathered together as one group. Click on the Select tool, click on any part of the drawing, then select Menu: Format|Explode to disassemble the group.

2. Use Zoom Window to gain a close-up view where the metal coping at the top of the wall is circled. Click on the Zoom Window tool in the View toolbar (right side of the screen), or select Menu: View|Zoom|Zoom Windows. Draw a selection rectangle around the circle at the top of the drawing.

Zoom window tool

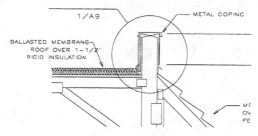

Close-up of the top of the drawing

3. From the menu, select Modify|Object Trim. Click on the circle to select it as the cutting edge for the trim operation.

4. Starting at any point along the circle, click on every object that intersects any portion of the circle. Be sure to click on the portion of each object lying *outside* the circle. Adjust the view as necessary to get a close-up view each object you trim. The lines and arcs of the roof membrane that intersect the circle can be trimmed, if you zoom in close enough to pick them individually. You will not be able to trim the rectangle that intersects the bottom of the circle. Leave it for the moment.

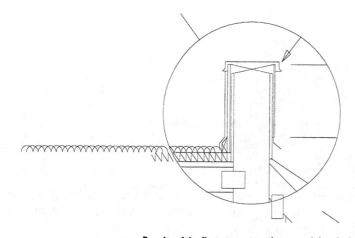

Results of the first attempt to trim around the circle

5. Click on the Select tool to end Object Trim.

6. Use Zoom Window to get a close-up view of the rectangle (bottom of circle) that did not trim.

7. Select the rectangle, then select Format|Explode from the menu. Click on the drawing area to deselect the rectangle.

8. From the menu, select Modify|Object Trim. Click on the circle to select is as the cutting edge.

9. Click on each line of the rectangle that intersects the circle. Be sure to click on the portions outside the circle. Select the Select tool to end Object Trim.

Remove Unnecessary Objects

You want every object that is part of the wall to stay in the circle, but the remaining pieces of the Leaders are not needed. (Leaders are lines—usually with arrows—that are used to label objects in a drawing. They will be covered in Chapter 11, Dimensioning.) Erase them now.

1. Choose the Select tool and <Shift-Click> on each line, arrow, etc., inside the circle but not a part of the wall detail. They are all found on the right side of the circle. Note that the line and the arrow near the top will need to be selected separately.

2. When all the non-wall objects are highlighted, press the <Delete> key to erase them.

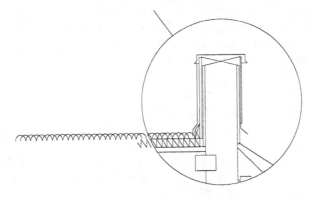

The leader lines inside the circle have been deleted

Selection Rectangle Options

The wall elements and the circle are now ready to be moved. But there are many objects close to the circle that make selecting the circle and its contents a challenge. Fortunately, there are a variety of selection options in TurboCAD.

So far in this guidebook, objects have been selected by one of two methods: clicking on them with the Select tool, or using the Select tool to draw a selection rectangle around the objects.

The selection rectangle gives different results, depending on whether Open Window mode is on or off. To change this option, click the right mouse button in the drawing area to open the local menu, then choose Open Window mode. If the menu item has a check next to it, the option is on; otherwise the option is off.

Local menu, showing open window mode checked

To use the selection rectangle with the Open Window option on, hold the left mouse button down and move the cursor, creating a rectangle over an area that contains *any part* of the objects that you want to select, then release the mouse button. If any portion of an object is inside the rectangle, the entire object will be selected. This includes nodes and vertices of the object.

To use the selection rectangle with the Open Window mode off, hold the left mouse button down and move the cursor, creating a rectangle over an area that contains the objects you want to select *in their entirety,* then release the mouse button. If any portion of an object is outside the rectangle, it will not be selected.

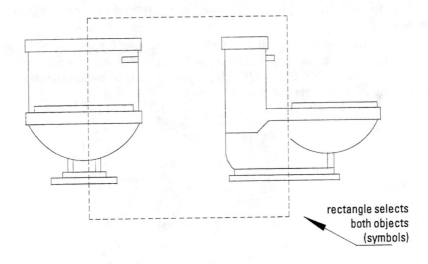

rectangle selects
both objects
(symbols)

Selection rectangle with Open Window option on

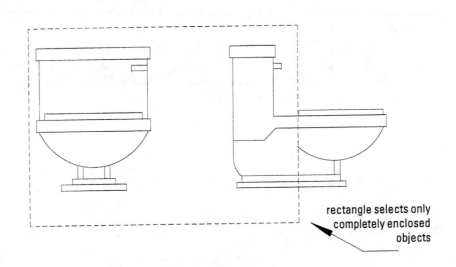

rectangle selects only
completely enclosed
objects

Selection rectangle with Open Window option off

Other Selection Options

Three additional selection methods are available from the Edit menu. Menu: Edit|Select All (keyboard shortcut: <Ctrl-A>) will select *every* object in the drawing. Menu: Edit|Select By has four options, Entity Type, Layer, Attribute, and Fence.

Select By Entity Type is used when you need to select all objects of a given type, such as Bezier curves. When the command is chosen, a dialog appears on-screen. Every possible type of object in TurboCAD is listed. You can use this dialog to select any type of object or combination of types, using common Windows list box selection techniques. If you wish to add objects of these types to a current selection, place a check in the Add to the Current Selection check box. If this box is not checked, then any currently selected items will be deselected as the new objects are selected. All objects in the drawing meeting the selection criteria will be highlighted.

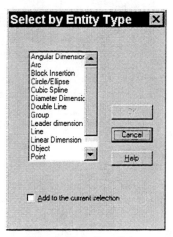

Select by Entity Type dialog

Select by Layer allows you to name one or more layers. When you do so, all objects on those layers will be selected. If you are organizing your drawings by layers (discussed in Chapter Nine), this selection option is very helpful. The next illustration shows the Select by Layer dialog for WDET.TCW.

Select by Layer dialog

Select By Fence lets you select a set of objects by drawing a polygon "fence" around them. The Open Window mode affects the action of the fence. If Open Window mode is on, any object that intersects or is inside the fence will be selected. If Open Window mode is off, only those objects completely inside the fence will be selected. Creating this fence is exactly like the using the Irregular Polygon drawing tool. You will use this tool in the steps below to select the circle and the details inside.

Select and Move Details

1. From the menu choose Edit|Select By|Fence.

2. Click on a point just outside the circle to start the selection fence.

3. Right-click to open the local menu. Make sure Open Window mode is off (not checked). If it is checked, click on it to shut it off.

4. Continue around the circle by clicking and moving the mouse. Each point you define will become a new vertex (corner) of an irregular polygon fence. A rubberband line will connect back to the origin of the fence as you draw. Make sure that any objects you wish to select are contained within the fence.

5. The area by the roof will be a tight fit. Use Zoom Window (or Zoom In, <Gray +>) interactively as you draw the fence if necessary to get a close-up of the right side of the circle.

6. Use Zoom Out (< Gray + > key on the numeric keypad or the Zoom Out icon in the View toolbar, right side of the screen) to get a wider view after drawing the fence through the area between the roof and the circle.

7. When you have worked all the way around the circle, right-click in the drawing area to access the local menu. Choose Finish to complete the fence and select the objects.

8. Click on Zoom Full View in the View menu to see the entire sheet.

9. Click (not on the reference point, but anywhere inside the selection window) and drag the selected objects (the circle and the top of the wall) to an open area on the sheet to the right.

10. Click anywhere in the drawing area (outside the selection window) to deselect the objects.

11. Use Zoom Window to gain a close-up of the objects.

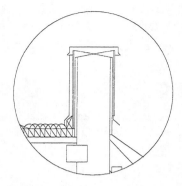

The circle and wall detail, separated from the rest of the drawing

Cut and Paste

Save the wall detail as a separate drawing, for use with the exercises in Chapter Twelve. Use Cut and Paste, two Edit menu commands exactly like their counterparts in many other Windows programs. Menu: Edit|Cut removes the selection to the Windows clipboard; Menu: Edit|Paste places a copy of the contents of the Windows clipboard.

Two features of the Windows clipboard should be remembered. First, it only holds one selection at a time. Second, when you use the Paste command in a Windows program, a *copy* of the item in the clipboard is retrieved. You can Paste the item an unlimited number of times.

If for some reason you don't want the wall detail removed from this drawing, substitute Copy (<Ctrl-C> or Menu: Edit|Copy) for Cut in the steps below.

1. Adjust the screen view so that the entire wall detail is visible.
2. Use any selection method you prefer to select the detail and the circle.
3. Press <Ctrl-X> or select Menu: Edit|Cut to remove the detail to the Windows clipboard.
4. From the menu, choose File|New. Select Normal as the template, and close the Setup Dialog if necessary.
5. Press <Ctrl-V> or select Menu: Edit|Paste.
6. Press <Ctrl-S> or select File|Save from the menu.
7. Name the new drawing CH12DET, and save it to the DRAWINGS folder or subdirectory. Fill in the details for the Summary Info dialog if you like.
8. Close the drawing (<Alt-F> <C> or Menu: File|Close). The original drawing returns to the screen.

NOTE: *It was not necessary to close the first drawing to create a new drawing. TurboCAD allows you to open many drawings at once. The limit depends on available memory.*

9.   There is no further need for CH7WDET in this exercise. Save and close the drawing.

Practice Makes Perfect

Take a few moments now to create a new drawing that looks like the one below. Use the Line, Double Line and Rectangle tools. Snap to Grid will make it easy to keep the lines straight.

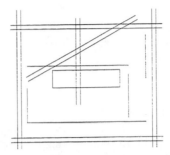

Draw this set of lines for the next exercise

After reading the descriptions of the various Modify commands below, take a few minutes to practice each command on some part of this drawing. Feel free to add or erase elements as necessary.

Chamfer and Fillet

When lines come together to make corners, you don't always want them to meet at a point. You may need to design an object with rounded corners, or you may need to create beveled corners. TurboCAD has a Modify command for each situation. These are Chamfer (for beveled corners) and Fillet (for rounded corners).

Chamfer

Chamfer joins two line segments or double line segments with a flattened (beveled) corner. The values used to calculate the chamfer appear in the Edit Bar when the command is active.

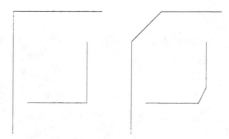

Chamfer before and after

To create a chamfer, you need to specify two distances in the Edit Bar, called Distance A and Distance B. Distance A is the distance from the point where the chamfer meets the first line clicked, to the point where the two lines intersect. Distance B is the corresponding distance on the second line. After specifying these distances in the Edit Bar, click on the two lines in the correct order: TurboCAD will draw a beveled corner at the intersection of the two lines.

Fillet

Fillet inserts an arc at the intersection of two nonparallel lines. These lines may meet at a common endpoint or they may overlap. The radius of the arc can be modified whenever the command is active by changing the value in the Edit Bar. By default, the radius is one inch.

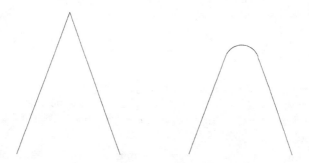

Fillet before and after

If the radius specified is too large for the arc to fit between the two lines, TurboCAD will be unable to perform the fillet and will display an error message.

 T ɪ ᴘ: *If fillet radius is set to 0, the fillet tool can be used to square off two lines that would intersect if connected. The tool extends each line, then inserts an arc of "zero" radius, i.e., no arc at all. This is an alternative to Meet 2 Lines.*

Meet 2 Lines

Use the Meet 2 Lines tool to shrink or extend two lines or double lines so that endpoints meet. This function automatically cleans up the corner formed by two double lines.

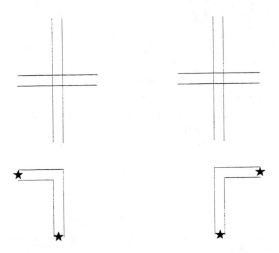

Two before-and-after examples of using Meet 2 Lines; stars identify click locations

To use this tool, simply click on the two lines. When the two lines are crossed, the two parts of the line that you click on will be preserved; the parts of the lines on the opposite side of the intersection will be trimmed.

Cleaning Double Line Intersections

Double lines can be handy for a variety of design applications. When two double lines cross, generally the intersection needs to be modified in some fashion. TurboCAD offers two tools specifically for cleaning double line intersections, T-Meet 2 Double Lines and Intersect 2 Double Lines.

Use T-Meet to form a "T" intersection of two double lines. The first line clicked will extend or shrink to meet the second double line and form the stem of the T.

The steps in using T-Meet are:

1. Select the tool (Menu: Modify|T-Meet 2 Double Lines).
2. Click on the line that will form the stem of the T.
3. Click on the line that will form the top of the T.

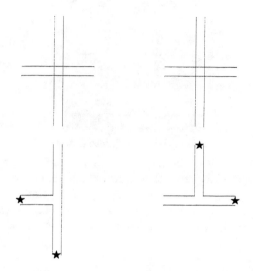

Two before-and-after examples using T-Meet 2 Double Lines; stars identify clicks

Use the Intersect 2 Double Lines tool to clean up the intersection of two double lines.

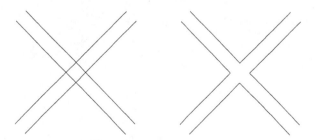

Before-and-after using Intersect 2 Double Lines

Both double line intersection tools have a special option available from the local menu (right mouse button) when the tool is active. The Cleanup option specifies whether or not a complete editing of the intersection will take place.

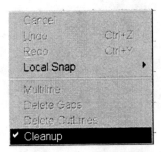

Local menu showing cleanup selected

If Cleanup is active for T-Meet, both sets of double lines will be open. If not, the first double line selected will be open (clean), the second will be blocked by the first line. If Cleanup is active for Intersect 2 Double lines, the intersection will be completely open, like two streets meeting at a four-way stop. If Cleanup is not active, the first double line selected will be open, blocking the second double line where they intersect.

An Infinite Number of Uses

The tools and commands available in the Edit and Modify menus can be used in an infinite number of drawing situations. Make a mental note to consider these tools as you start to create your own drawings.

Not every command in these two menus has been covered in this chapter. Some have already been used, and some will be used in upcoming chapters, especially Chapter Ten.

8
Text in the CAD Drawing

Providing Context for Images

Text plays a key role in design drawings. It provides context, bridging the gap between verbal and visual communications. Place the word *Kitchen* in a room of a floor plan, and it is immediately clear to the reader that all objects in the room are appliances, cupboards, etc. The one word gives enough context without having to name the objects individually. Anyone looking at the drawing can "read" the objects correctly.

The use of text is an important part of creating successful CAD drawings, as important as any line in the drawing. Placing text in a drawing should not be an afterthought in the drafting process.

An Extra Benefit for Graphic Designers

Text placement tools are available in TurboCAD because they are essential to CAD. Whether you draw homes, stage lighting schematics or pistons, you need text. But the combination of text and CAD tools makes it possible to use TurboCAD as a graphic design tool. There are ways to manipulate text in TurboCAD to create special effects otherwise possible only in expensive professional graphic design and publishing software.

The methods of text manipulation discussed in this chapter can be applied to either drafting or graphic design with equal flexibility. Chapter Twelve will cover the use of other non-geometric objects for visual detailing in TurboCAD drawings.

Text and Professional Drafting Standards

Take a look at the letters that make up the words you are reading right now. Examine their shape, their width, their height. Look for common elements in the letters. These elements define these particular letters as part of a *font,* a complete character set in a distinctive style. Windows uses a technology called TrueType to generate fonts. The Windows operating system ships with several TrueType fonts, and hundreds more are available for purchase. TurboCAD can place any installed TrueType font in a drawing.

What is a TrueType font? In order to understand the differences between TrueType fonts and other typefaces, lets look briefly at the history of text in CAD software.

The first generation of popular DOS-based CAD programs each used a different method to represent text. Basically, each letter was a tiny drawing, consisting of lines, arcs and sometimes curves. The typefaces (fonts) used by these programs were copies of typefaces used in manual drafting, where every letter had to be created by hand by the draftsman. Each CAD program had its own technology for generating text. Typefaces created for one program could not be used by another, unless special conversion software was available.

Before CAD, the various drafting professions (primarily architecture and engineering) had developed standards for the appearance of text in drawings. As CAD began to replace manual drafting, the old standards for typefaces remained in place. But the introduction of Windows (and to a lesser extent, the Macintosh) has caused a revolution in drafting standards. The ability to use "real" fonts (as used in publishing) has caused many a drafting professional to drop the old-style stick fonts for a modern typeset appearance. But not all drafting professionals have adopted the new look for their drawings. To meet the needs of traditional draftsmen using modern tools, TrueType fonts are available for purchase that look like the old-style stick lettering. If you will be creating drawings that must meet specific professional standards, be sure to find out if you are restricted to the use of certain approved typefaces, or if you have the freedom to use any legible typeface. If there are restrictions, try to find out if an appropriate TrueType font is available.

The advantage of TrueType fonts, and the primary reason they have become a standard element in the Windows environment, is their flexibility. TrueType fonts are scalable to any size without a loss of resolution. Embedded into the architecture of each letter is the programming instructions that allow a Windows program to modify the size of the letter as required. The internal definition of the letter provides the necessary algorithms to shape the letter correctly at any size required.

Not only do the various drafting professions have standards about the use of fonts, there are also standards about the size of type in drawings. These standards vary with the profession, and it is beyond the scope of this book to try to teach the various rules. TurboCAD makes it easy to adjust text to any height, using the drawing units (English or metric) instead of *points,* the text measurement system used in typography and graphic design.

NOTE: *If you are familiar with points as a unit of measurement for type, you can use points instead of inches (or fractions thereof) by placing your text using Paper Space instead of World Space. The Text Format toolbar, if active, provides the opportunity to set type size in points.*

If you don't have a specific set of professional guidelines to go by, uses these rules of thumb as you create working drawings:

- Use only one font whenever possible. Use two fonts only if there are two distinct types of objects being labeled.

- Avoid novelty fonts for working drawings. If you don't have specialty fonts for drafting, stick to Ariel, Courier New and Times New Roman.

- When printed to an 8 1/2" x 11" sheet, the largest characters should never be more than 1/4" tall.

- If you are familiar with points as a measurement for text, remember that 72 points equals one inch. When you are working in World Space, TurboCAD uses the current unit of measurement for text, not points. If you want 18-point text in the drawing, you would use 1/4" text (18 divided by 72). As explained above, you may want to change to Paper Space and use points directly.

- If both text and dimensions are used, the dimension text should be no taller than 75 percent of the height of text used to label major objects.

- Leader text should be the same size as dimension text. (Dimensions and leaders are covered in Chapter Eleven.)

Placing Text in a Drawing

The basics of text placement in TurboCAD are simple. Before you start with the exercises in this chapter, add the Text Format toolbar to your desktop. Select Menu: View|Toolbars. The Program Setup dialog will appear. Click on the Desktop tab, then click on Text Format in the list of available toolbars. When you click the OK button, the Text Format toolbar will appear on-screen.

Follow these steps whenever you need to place text in a drawing:

1. Activate the Text tool, in the Insert Entity toolbar.

Text tool icon

2. If you wish to set the font, size, and attributes of text (such as underlining or italic) prior to typing, choose settings from the Text Format toolbar. As an alternative, you can set text properties by right-clicking on the Text tool, then changing the properties in the Text property sheet that appears.

3. Click in the drawing area at the point where you want to place your text. Any snap command may be used to identify this location.

4. Type the text that you want to place, using the <Backspace> key to make corrections. Press <Shift> + <Enter> to add a new line of text. To finish the text, press <Enter>, or right-click and choose Finish from the local menu.

Using these steps as a guide, place the phrase (include the misspellings) *Drawin by TurbuCAD* in a new drawing. Use the Text Format toolbar or the Text property sheet (shown below) to set text properties as:

- Font: Courier New
- Height: 0.5 in.
- Style: Bold
- Justification: Left

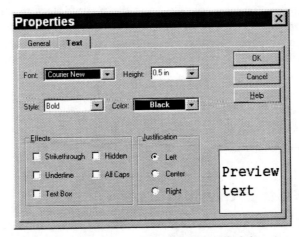

Text properties dialog, with settings as described above

Make sure either No Snap or Snap to Grid is active, or you will not be able to place text in the new drawing.

Editing Text in a Drawing

Once text has been placed in a drawing, it may be edited for content as necessary.

1. Change to the Select tool, and select the line of text. Use either a selection rectangle or click on the line of text.
2. Right-click on the drawing area to summon the local menu, or double-click on the line of text to be edited.
3. Select Properties. The Properties dialog will appear. The selected text will be highlighted in the Attribute field.

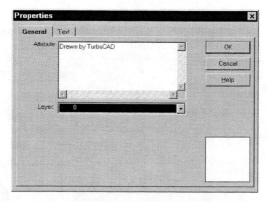

Properties dialog, with the text phrase visible in the attributes field

4. Click somewhere on the line of text to insert a text placement cursor. Use the arrow keys and <Backspace> (or <Delete>) to change *Drawin* to *Drawn, by* to *In*, and *TurbuCAD* to *TurboCAD*. When finished, click on OK. (The <Enter> key will not work in this situation as an alternative to clicking the OK button.)

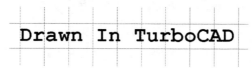

Corrected phrase as it appears on the drawing sheet

Reformatting Text in a Drawing

It is OK to change your mind about the format of the text you have placed in the drawing. TurboCAD allows you to adjust all text properties after text has been placed in a drawing.

1. Select the text (if not still selected from the previous exercise).
2. Right-click to summon the local menu. Select Properties.
3. Click the Text tab.
4. Change Style to Italic.
5. Change Height to 0.67 in.
6. Select Underline in Effects.
7. Select Gray in Color. (The complete list of colors available depends on your computer hardware.)
8. Click OK to finish.

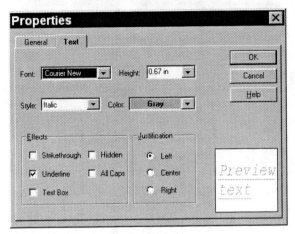

Text properties with changes made

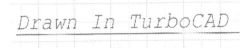

Text revisions as they appear on the drawing sheet

Manipulating Text

So far we have edited the text and changed its properties, similar to doing it in a word processor. TurboCAD sees the text as a TrueType font, and treats it accordingly.

 NOTE: *The use of text is the first example in this book of placing non-geometric entities in a drawing. Chapter Twelve covers the use of other objects that do not conform to the rules of geometry.*

TurboCAD 3 for Windows has many options for manipulating text, based on the principle that you can edit or modify the text as:

- a TrueType font
- a group of polygons
- individual polygons
- multilines and fill patterns

As a TrueType font, not only can you edit the text and change its properties, but also you can select the text and stretch it or rotate it by manipulating the selection rectangle.

If you want more freedom to manipulate the text graphically, you need to explode the text to turn the characters into irregular polygons. The first time you do this, you will turn the text object into a group of polygons. If you explode the text a second time, it will ungroup so that each individual character can be manipulated as a polygon. You can resize, stretch, move, flip, or rotate each individual character in Select Edit mode. You can change the pen, brush pattern, or other properties of the multiline by double-clicking on the selection and changing the settings in the Properties dialog.

Align Existing Text to a Line

While the text is still a TrueType font, it is possible to align it to an existing line in the drawing. You can move existing text, or place new text along a line as you type it.

Use the text created above to practice aligning to a line.

1. Select the text. Drag it to the bottom of the Paper (to get it out of the way), by dragging anywhere inside the selection rectangle.

2. Click No Snap, then select the Line tool and draw a diagonal line from roughly the lower left corner of the Paper to the upper right.

3. Select the line, then select Menu: View|Selection Info.

4. Note the value given for Angle. In the illustration the angle is 32.59 degrees; your value may vary. Close the Selection Info dialog (or drag it out of the way if you don't think you can remember the value).

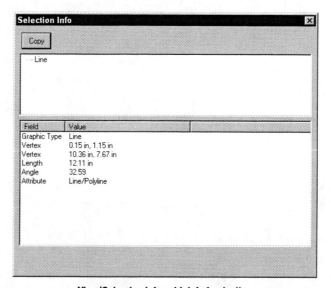

View|Selection Info, with info for the line

5. Select the text. Press the <Tab> key until Rotation is selected in the Edit Bar. Type the value noted above and press <Enter> to rotate the text to this angle.

6. Select Nearest Entity Point from the Snaps toolbar. No other snap should be active.

Nearest entity point snap tool

7. The text should still be selected. Move the cursor over the reference point in the center of the selection rectangle. Press the <Ctrl> key. When the four-sided arrow changes to a hand, click to pick up the reference point.

 NOTE: *Moving a selected object's reference point was introduced in Chapter Three.*

8. Move the cursor to the lower left handle and click to place the reference point.

9. The cursor reverts to a four-sided arrow. Drag the text to the lower end of the line. Click to attach the reference point to the endpoint. Click anywhere in the drawing area to deselect the text.

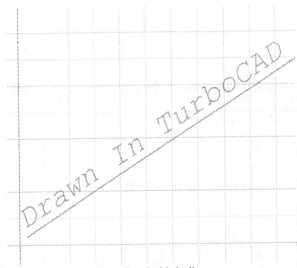

Text aligned with the line

 TIP: *Manipulating text in TurboCAD can cause stray pixels to appear on-screen as you work. Press <F5> to force a screen redraw at any time.*

If you know that you need to place text at an angle, and you already know the angle of rotation, change the angle in the Edit Bar after selecting the Text Insert tool but before clicking to set the location of the text.

Align New Text to a Line

The next sequence uses the External Text Alignment command. This feature provides precise control over how text is aligned relative to the point where it is inserted in the drawing. To activate these options, select the text tool, right-click in the drawing area, and then choose Align. The command will be followed by two capital letters that vary, depending on the current alignment setting.

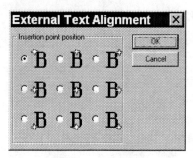

External text align dialog

The star next to each alignment setting shows you graphically how the text is positioned relative to the insertion point. There are three vertical positions (top, center, bottom) and three horizontal positions (left, right, middle), for nine total settings. When you reopen the local menu with the Text tool active, the letters next to Align represent the current setting. TL, for example, means the insertion point will be at the top left corner of the text.

1. Erase the existing text or drag it aside.
2. Select the Text tool, then select Snap Vertex.
3. Click on the left endpoint of the line and type the sentence *New text at any angle is easy.* Do *not* press <Enter>.
4. Right-click to summon the local menu. Select Align. The External Text Align dialog will appear.
5. Click on the radio button for bottom left (the bottom left option in the dialog).
6. Click on OK.
7. Press the <Tab> key until angle is highlighted in the Edit Bar. Type the angle of the line, and press <Enter>. The text will rotate to the new angle.

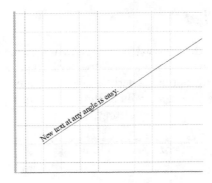

Text at new angle along line

Align Text to an Arc or Circle

If you really want to get fancy, you can align text to an arc or circle, real or imagined. The sequence below will align to an existing circle. To align text in a radial pattern without aligning to a specific circle or arc, skip the step that places the text character on the entity. For this example, use the phrase *Love makes the world go around.*

 NOTE: *This technique uses Fit Radial Copy, introduced in Chapter Six.*

1. Erase all existing objects on screen. Draw a large circle.

2. Count the number of characters in the phrase to be placed in the drawing. Be sure to count spaces as characters. If you plan to align text around the circumference of a circle, count two or three extra characters for space at the end. Adding two extra spaces (and no period) to *Love makes the world go around* totals 32 characters.

3. Select the Text tool. Click Quadrant Snap in the Snaps toolbar.

Quadrant snap tool

4. Click on the top of the circle and type L, the first letter of the phrase. Press <Enter>.

5. Click on the Select tool, and select the letter.

6. From the menu, choose Edit|Copy Entities|Fit Radial Copy.

7. Click on Arc Center in the Snaps toolbar. Deselect Quadrant Snap.

Arc center snap tool

8. Click on the circumference of the circle. The Fit Radial Copy will then snap to the center of the circle.

9. Press the <Tab> key until Sets is highlighted in the Edit Bar. Type the number of characters you need (32 in this example).

10. Press the <Tab> key again to highlight Angle. Type 360 and press <Enter>. The letter L will be copied around the circle, making a total of 32 copies.

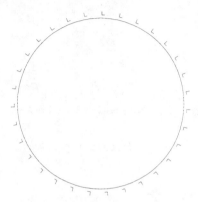

32 copies of 'L' around a circle

11. Decide where on the circle you want the phrase to begin. In this example, start on the upper left side of the circle (where 10 would be on a clock).

12. Select the letter *one character clockwise* from the starting point of the phrase, then double-click on the letter to access the Properties dialog. Click on the general tab if not already active.

13. The letter will be highlighted in the Properties dialog. Type *o*, the second character of the phrase. Click OK.

14. Select the next letter, right-click, select Properties, and type *v*, the third letter of the phrase. Click OK.

15. Repeat the process to change every letter in sequence.

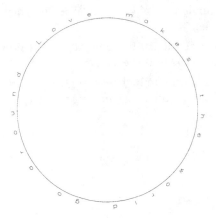

Finished circle with "Love makes the world go around" on it

 TIP: *To place spaces between the words, don't bother right-clicking for the Properties dialog. Just delete the character.*

Manipulating Text as Graphic Elements

It was not necessary to explode the text in any of the techniques already given. If you want to create special graphic effects with text, you must explode the characters first.

1. Delete all objects on the screen, or save your work and start a new drawing.
2. Select the Text tool. In the Text Format toolbar, change the font to Ariel, the size to 1 in., and select Bold.

Text toolbar with settings as described

3. Select Snap to Grid from the Snaps toolbar.
4. Click to the left of center on the Paper, and type your initials or *TCD* (for TurboCAD Designs). Press <Enter>.
5. Switch to the Select tool. Select the text, then select Menu: Format|Explode.
6. With the letters still selected, use Explode again. Then click anywhere in the drawing area.
7. Each letter is now a separate object. Select the first letter.
8. Right-click to summon the local menu. Select Node Edit.

In Node Edit mode, you can reshape entities or objects by directly manipulating particular points, called *nodes*. Nodes are available on most TurboCAD objects and entities by selecting the object and selecting Node Edit from the local menu. (Node Edit was introduced in Chapter Six, and will be covered in more detail in both Chapter Ten and Chapter Twelve.) Nodes should not be confused with the handles on a selection rectangle. Nodes are points found on the object. Nodes identify locations of geometric significance on an object or entity, and are used by TurboCAD to define the object mathematically in the drawing database stored on disk. (*Drawing database* is the technical term for what you would normally call the drawing file.)

9. Experiment by dragging various nodes on each of the letters, to reshape the letters. To switch back to select edit (the mode with the selection rectangle), right-click to summon the local menu and choose Select Edit.

Node Edit was used to modify these characters after they were exploded

Import Text from Other Applications

If you need a large block of text in a drawing, or if the text you need already exists in another document, you can import the text into a TurboCAD drawing. There are two methods available:

• Menu: Edit|Paste, which pastes any data that has been previously copied or cut to the Windows clipboard.

• Menu: Edit|Paste Special, which also pastes any data that has been previously copied or cut to the Windows clipboard. Paste Special offers the ability to use OLE, Object Linking and Embedding, a Windows function. Menu: Edit|Paste Special is covered in Chapter Twelve.

Using Menu: Edit|Paste, it is possible to bring in text, bitmap images, or metafile graphic images from other Windows applications.

Use Menu: Edit|Paste in the exercise below to import text from TurboCAD Help into a drawing.

1. Delete all objects on the screen, or save and open a new drawing.

2. Select the text tool, so that the Text Format toolbar is active. Change the text size to .25 in or smaller.

3. From the menu, select Help|TurboCAD Help Topics.

4. Select Search. Type *Paste* and press <Enter>.

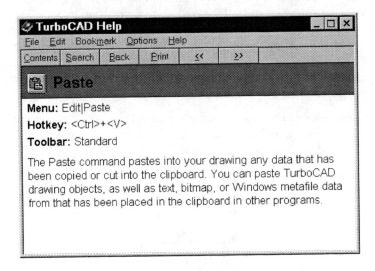

TurboCAD help screen for the Paste command

5. Move the cursor onto the body of the text. Highlight the first three lines (Menu:, Hotkey:, and Toolbar:)

6. From the Help screen menu, select Edit|Copy, or press <Ctrl> + <C> to copy the highlighted text.

7. Double-click on the Control Menu Box to close the Help screen.

8. Back in TurboCAD, select Menu: Edit|Paste, or press <Ctrl> + <V>. The text from the help screen will appear in the drawing with a selection rectangle. Click anywhere on the drawing area to deselect.

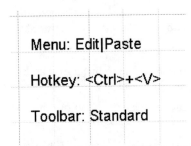

Text from TurboCAD Help pasted into a drawing

The Best of Both Worlds

Some people relate better to graphic images and visual communications. Others relate better to words. TurboCAD bridges the gap by offering a robust set of text tools. Not only can you annotate technical drawings to provide context and complete explanation, but you can use TurboCAD as a graphic design sketchpad.

Some of the features and concepts introduced in this chapter will be revisited later. Text is a non-geometric object in TurboCAD, and has aspects in common with other objects such as hatches, color fills, bitmaps, and metafiles.

9

File and Data Management

Organizing the Information You Create

First and foremost, CAD programs are not about pictures. They are about *data*. A design is the visual representation of information — data. The CAD program helps you organize this information into a recognizable visual form. Using drafting and editing tools, you create specific images that convey specific meaning.

In addition to the geometric entities and other objects you draw, TurboCAD offers other ways of organizing and displaying the information in a drawing. This chapter covers the fundamentals of organizing and managing the varieties of data generated by a designer or drafter.

Comparing Drawings to Documents

To understand how a drawing conveys information, compare a TurboCAD drawing to a typical document made with a word processor.

In the document, the basic element is the character. In English, characters are the 26 letters, capital and lower case, plus punctuation and math symbols. In the drawing, the basic element is the point, a geometric element that has position but no size.

In a document, we combine groups of characters to create a word. By itself, each character has no inherent meaning. But when combined to make words (or equations, if dealing with math), each grouping carries an idea. Therefore, we must be careful when we put characters together. For example, *unite* and *untie* use exactly the same letters, in almost the same order, but their definitions are opposites.

In a TurboCAD drawing, the counterpart of a word is the entity. As defined in Chapter Two, lines, arcs, circles, and the other primitive objects in TurboCAD are all entities. They are carefully arranged groups of points, and this arrangement determines their geometric definition. For example, a circle is defined by the location of its center and its radius. All the points on the circle then "line up" so that they are exactly the same distance from the center.

Words and equations in a document may be given emphasis. In this book, for example, we make use of Capitalization, **bold type,** *italic type,* and `changing fonts` to give emphasis. Other forms of emphasis in a document may be variations of font styles, the use of small capital letters, changes in type size, and if available, color. Each of these variations in emphasis is an attribute, not of the word itself, but of how the word appears in print.

It is also possible to emphasize entities in TurboCAD, with the use of such attributes as color, line pattern, pen width, and the layer the object resides on. Each of these elements will be defined in this chapter, and suggestions for use offered.

Words combine, with or without emphasis, to form a sentence. Sentences combine to form a paragraph, and paragraphs to form the document. Each level imparts information, and as the parts become a whole the author presents the message.

In TurboCAD, entities combine to form objects, objects may be formed into groups, and both are presented together to form a total concept, the design message. In both the document and the drawing, the full intent of the designer comes through when the entities are seen as a unified, single work.

A reader may analyze some parts of a document separately. For example, a memorandum from a company CEO may outline five steps to be taken by various departments. Readers from each of these departments will read the entire memo, but will pay especially close attention to steps involving their particular department.

Most CAD drawings will also be analyzed on a piece-by-piece basis. Consider how the drawings for a new house will be used. The appliance delivery crew will look to see where appliances are to be installed, plumbers will look at the plans for the plumbing, and electricians, carpet installers and other subcontractors will focus on the parts of the drawing requiring their attention. All will look at how their part of the job fits into the complete design. This detailed analysis of a CAD drawing can be made easier by organizing and highlighting information in the drawing.

CAD Management Systems

For each entity you draw in TurboCAD, you can define:

- Pen color
- Pen width
- Line pattern
- Dash Scale
- Alignment
- Layer
- Width scaling

In addition, each object can be given its own label or explanation, known as an *attribute.*

There can be a virtually infinite number of colors, widths, patterns, dash scales and layers. If you have only been thinking of CAD drawings in terms of thin solid black lines, this sudden availability of infinite variety may be a little overwhelming.

Most experienced drafters and designers rely on a CAD management system to guide them in the selection of these variables. The system is either the result of personal decisions, company standards, the advice of a professional organization, or tradition. You should seek out examples of standards that are relevant to your situation, and begin to use them in your design projects. Lacking the availability of such standards, you can still organize your drawings using color, line type, and the other options. In a construction plan, for example, you could use color to identify various raw materials such as wood, masonry, and sheet rock. Wiring could be in one color (or 120v in one color, 220v in another), as could plumbing.

Various elements of information management and presentation discussed below will be accompanied by a brief hands-on section. Instead of taking the time to draw a variety of objects, and then modify their color, layer data, etc., the drawing TECHNIC1.TCW, included with your copy of TurboCAD, will be used for exploring some of these options.

Properties of Entities

TurboCAD provides a variety of ways to display and record entities in a drawing. The available settings are controlled in the Properties dialog, available from the menu at Format|Properties. This menu item is not available unless an entity in the drawing is selected; the settings you see in the Properties dialog belong to the selected entity.

For all entities, the Properties dialog has three sections, each called a Properties sheet:

- General
- Pen
- Brush

Additional property sheets for Double Line, Curve, Point, Text and the various dimensions styles, appear in the Properties Dialog only if one of these entities is selected.

General Properties

The General properties sheet lets you select a layer and add an *attribute* to the entity. A complete discussion of layers follows shortly. A text attribute is a brief explanation that you can link to the entity. For example, if a polygon represents a bolt, you can select the polygon and list a part number or size as the text attribute for the polygon. If a specific text attribute is not created by the user, the name of the entity (line, polygon, curve, etc.) will appear.

The Selection Info palette, introduced in Chapter Six, will display the text attribute of a selected entity. By clicking the Copy button in the Selection Info palette, the text attribute (and all the other data associated with the entity) is copied to the Windows clipboard.

1. Start TurboCAD and open the drawing TECHNIC1.TCW, in the \SAMPLES folder or subdirectory.

2. Select the bottom line from the side view (the side view is the object in the top left quadrant of the drawing).

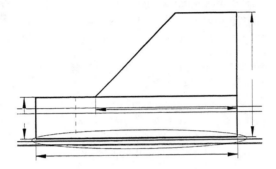

The line to select is circled

3. Right-click to summon the local menu. Click on Properties.

4. The General Properties sheet appears, with a text cursor blinking in the Attribute field. Type *Baseline, side view.* Do not press <Enter> or click on OK yet.

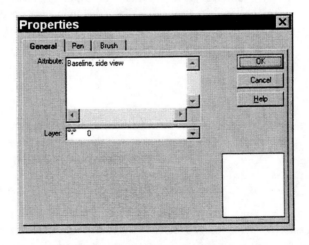

General property sheet with attribute phrase

Pen Properties

The Pen properties sheet controls the look of lines in the drawing. In this context, *lines* means all geometric entities, not just objects created by the Line tools. The main elements are pattern, color, and thickness.

Twenty-six line patterns are available in TurboCAD. The ten most commonly used in all the various drafting professions are shown below. The others 16 patterns represent variations on these ten basic patterns. These line patterns are common to most CAD programs:

Line Pattern name	Representation
Continuous	———————
Border	– – – – – – – –
Center	— · — · — · —
Dashdot	– · – · – · – ·
Dashed	– – – – – – – –
Divide	– · · – · · –
Dot	· · · · · · · · · · · ·
Hidden	- - - - - - - - - - - -
Phantom	— · · — · · —
$Auxiliary	············

Check the Alignment box if you want the line pattern to align itself so that the corners of rectangles and polygons are always solid, no matter how the line pattern is used.

The number of colors available in your copy of TurboCAD depends on the capabilities of your computer hardware. The software receives information on the number of available colors from the Windows operating system.

 NOTE: *You can create new colors using the Color Palette property sheet, Meni: Tools/Color Palette.*

The Dash Scale setting is used to modify the scale of a pen's dot-dash pattern. For example, if you set the scale at .5 (instead of the default, 1), the dots and dashes will be half the default scale, and the dot-dash pattern will be repeated twice as often. This is an essential feature for creating complicate site plans, which require a wide variety of line types that are essentially the same two or three line patterns at various scales.

Width Scaling determines whether the width of the line will be scaled, or remain the same size, when you zoom in and out of the drawing. If you select Device, the width will be scaled relative to your computer screen and printer, and will remain the same size at any magnification. If you choose World, then the width will be scaled with your drawing and will change size as soon as you zoom in and out. This setting also applies to the size of the elements in the pen's dot-dash pattern.

The Width box controls the pen width. You can choose a listed size, or type in a value.

Continuing on with the tutorial:

5. Click on the Pen tab.

6. Use the selection arrow for the Color field to select blue as the new color.

7. Use the selection arrow for the Width field to select 0.05 in as the new width.

8. Click the OK button to close the Properties dialog.

9. Click anywhere in the drawing area to deselect the line. Notice how it changes to match the new settings in the Properties dialog.

Brush Properties

The Brush property sheet is used to control solid color fills and hatch patterns in closed entities such as circles and polygons. Solid color fills and hatch patterns are discussed in Chapter Twelve.

Using Layers in a Drawing

TurboCAD drawings can be organized into layers. They are virtual levels in a drawing, analogous to acetate sheets (overlays) in traditional drafting. Each layer is a separate drawing "surface." When printed, a drawing may display all layers, or any combination chosen by the designer.

Layers give you the advantage of sorting objects in your drawing. You can use layers to organize by the type of object, by order of creation, or by any other method that suits the way you work. You can then place each category of object on a separate layer of the drawing, so that you can work on one layer of objects at a time. Layers can be visible or not visible, editable or not editable. If you want to view only a subset of the objects in your drawing, set the layers you want to see as visible, and set all other layers to invisible. Setting layers to non-editable makes it possible to protect objects on those layers from unintended change while working on another layer of the drawing.

Consider the possibilities you have in using layers. You can:

- Arrange levels of detail layer-by-layer, so that one layer shows basic elements (exterior walls), another layer reveals an additional level of detail (interior partitions), a third layer holds yet a smaller level of detail (furnishings for a room), and so on.

- Divide phases of construction into separate layers, by trade or subcontractor.

- Place object dimensions on a layer separate from the object, allowing you to print a version of the design without size and scale specifications. A sales representative for an office workstation manufacturer could use this feature to hide the measurements in a bid drawing, so competitors can't benefit from his measurements if he leaves a printed copy of the drawing with a customer.

- If you develop a scheme for the organization of a drawing using layers, you may be able to print many types of drawings from the same file. For example, you could print a floor plan as a foundation plan, a dimensioned floor plan, a furniture plan, or a presentation floor plan, depending on which layers you turn on and off.

Several professional societies have published layer organization plans for their membership, the most notable being American Institute of Architects (AIA) and the Army Corps of Engineers.

Using Layers to Force Standards

TurboCAD allows you to set a default line color and line style for a layer. While it isn't mandatory, setting line color and/or line style by layer forces a plan of organization into the drawing. To take best advantage of assigning line settings to layers, you would need to create (or adopt an existing) line type and color plan for your work.

Follow the steps below to assign line and color standards to a new layer.

1. Start a new drawing. When the Template dialog appears, click Cancel.
2. A second dialog appears, informing you that TurboCAD will use the defaults used in the program's INI file to establish defaults. Click OK.
3. From the menu, select Tools|Layer.
4. Type 001 in the Name field. Click on New to make 001 the name of a new layer.
5. Select Red from the Color field.
6. Click on the Selection arrow for Line Style, and select the second line style shown (Border).
7. Click on the Name field, and type 002. Click on New to make 002 the name of a new layer.
8. Select Green from the color field.
9. Click on OK.

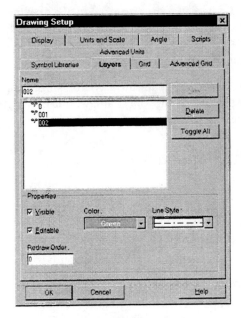

Setting standards for new layers

Tool-based Property Selection

The first set of hands-on steps made changes to the properties of an existing entity. Modifying the properties of every object after it has been drawn would be a slow way to work. TurboCAD allows you to set the properties of objects *before* they are drawn, by linking properties to a specific tool. This way you can draw objects to your CAD management standards from the start, eliminating the need to reedit according to your standards. This can be a great time-saver, especially if you create a template to store your property standards. Creating new templates is covered in Chapter Thirteen.

If you want to use layers to organize your drawing standards, set the tool to the layer. If you want to draw on any layer with specific properties, set the tool to the properties before you draw. Right-click on a tool button to establish properties. If the color and line-style properties of objects on a layer are set to By Layer, they will have the color and line style assigned to the layer.

Tool-based property selection is not unique to TurboCAD, but the majority of CAD programs on the market do not use this method. Instead, layers, colors, line types, etc. are all set independently, and must be kept track of separately. Tool-based property selection allows for a quick integration of all aspects of CAD management.

The Layers property sheet allows you to create new layers, set the properties of layers, and delete layers. To create a new layer, type a name for the layer in the Name text box, then click the New button. The new layer name will appear in the Layers dialog list box.

The current drawing layer is the layer on which any new objects that you create or insert will reside. To set the current drawing layer, use the Property Toolbar. (Use Menu: View|Toolbars to add the Property Toolbar to your TurboCAD desktop.)

Property Toolbar

You can set the properties of a layer using the controls in the Properties area of the Layers dialog. Any changes you make apply to the layer that is currently selected in the Layers dialog list box.

1. Right-click on the line tool. Click on the Pen tab to access the Pen properties sheet.

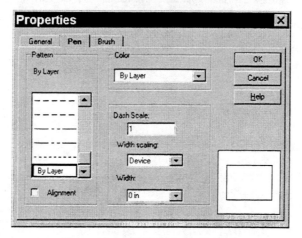

The pen properties sheet for the line tool

2. Use the scroll bars to select By Layer in the Pattern field.
3. Use the Selection Arrow to select By Layer in the Color field.
4. Click on the General tab.
5. In the Layer field, select 001.
6. Click the OK button to close the Properties dialog.
7. Click on the line tool, then draw two separate lines anywhere on screen. The lines should appear red and in the border line pattern style.

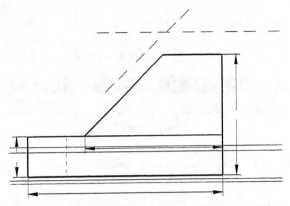

Two new lines in BORDER style have been added to the drawing

8. Right-click on the Line tool. Select the General tab, and set the layer to 002.

9. In the Attribute field, type *Sample Green Lines*. Click on the OK button.

10. Draw two more lines anywhere on screen. The lines should appear green.

Setting the Default Properties of a Tool

When you set the default properties of a tool, all subsequent entities drawn with that tool will have the settings you specified, until you explicitly change them. To access the default properties, either right-click on the tool icon as mentioned above, or activate the tool and then choose Menu: Format|Properties.

Setting the Properties of Selected Objects

The Properties dialog is context-sensitive — when you open it, the dialog will show the set of property sheets appropriate to the objects selected. If you select a double line, then bring up the Properties dialog, the dialog will contain the Double Line property sheet.

You can use this dialog to set the default properties for a drawing tool; or to set the individual properties of a particular object or set of objects.

The Property Toolbar

In addition to using the Properties dialog, the Properties toolbar is available to set and change properties. The Property Toolbar does not appear on screen when you launch TurboCAD, you must select it from either Menu: View|Toolbars, or Menu: Tools|Desktop. Check "Property" in the list of available toolbars, and it will appear on the desktop.

If no objects are currently selected, the settings on the Property toolbar apply to the active drawing tool. If you activate any single line tool and then change the settings on the Property toolbar, the settings will apply to all objects drawn with any single line tool.

NOTE: *You should always remove the Properties toolbar from the desktop if you are going to run a TurboCAD script. If the Properties toolbar is visible when a script is running, the screen redraws to display the property of every item affected by the script. This slows the script down considerably.*

Choosing Among Symbols, Blocks, and Groups

Chapter Three introduced The First Law of CAD: Only draw an object once. In subsequent tutorials symbols and groups have been introduced as ways to organize related entities that together form an object in your drawing. There is a third way to link entities, by saving them as a block. Blocks are similar to groups in that they consist of a collection of entities unified into a single object. When a block is created, the data that defines the block is stored in a block library. The block library is part of the drawing file. When more than one copy of any particular block is used in a drawing, TurboCAD refers back to the original definition of the block to draw each additional insertion.

The obvious questions are, which ones do you use, and when do you use them? Here are some guidelines:

- If you will be drawing an object, and using that object repeatedly in the drawing, save the object as a block. An example would be a bolt. Only one definition of the object needs to be stored in RAM memory as you work, saving time during redraw. This also helps keep the file size smaller.

- If the object will be used on a long-term basis, in project after project, save it as a symbol. An example would be a sofa in plan view. It will reside on the hard drive as a separate file. Related symbols can be saved in common file folders (Windows 95) or subdirectories (Windows 3.1).

- If you have drawn an object unique to your current drawing, link the entities that define the object as a group. This will make it easier to move the object. Groups are easier to manipulate than separate entities if you use the Align command.

- If you aren't sure whether to use a block or a group in a given situation, go with blocks. Blocks offer a rotation field option when selected. Also, the next version of TurboCAD is scheduled to add new features to the block option.

Organized Details Are Useful Details

This chapter provides an overview of the tools and procedures available in TurboCAD to organize and manage the information you generate as you draw. In essence, TurboCAD is a visual database, since it provides tools and procedures to create, organize and retrieve specific kinds of visual information. As you continue to practice and use TurboCAD, take the time to add an organizing plan to your work. Consider how to use various colors, layers, line types and other aspects of CAD management to your work. If you can, get a copy of the CAD management guidelines from a professional organization.

10
Drawing Techniques Part Two

Arcs, Circles and Curves

This chapter continues the discussion of geometric construction introduced in Chapter Six. In Chapter Six we emphasized straight lines; now we will concern ourselves with the use of arcs, circles, curves and related objects. The techniques and ideas presented in this chapter apply in a wide variety of situations, and are useful in all professional applications.

This chapter features a mix of short tutorials that focus on the use of one particular tool with a slightly longer tutorial that provides an opportunity to use several commands and tools together.

Basic definitions for geometric objects were provided in Chapter Six. If you are not familiar with any of the terms used in this chapter, refer back for the definitions.

Arc Placement Guidelines

TurboCAD offers eleven ways to draw an arc — including three elliptical arc tools. These tools, and their functions, are:

Tool	Action
Arc Center and Radius	Specify a radius point (center point) and a point on the circumference.
Concentric Arc	Draw arcs that share a common center
Double Point	Define the endpoints of the arc's diameter
Arc Tangent to Arc	Draw a circular arc tangent to a circle or to another arc.
Arc Tangent to Line	Draw a circular arc tangent to a line.

Tool	Action
Arc Tangent to 3 Arcs	Draw a circular arc tangent to three other arcs or circles.
Start/Included/End (1-2-3)	Define an arc by its starting point (1), a point on its perimeter (2), and its ending point (3).
Start/End/Included (1-3-2)	Define an arc by starting point (1), ending point, and then by a point on its perimeter (2).
Elliptical Arc	Draw an elliptical arc by defining its bounding rectangle.
Rotated Elliptical Arc	Draw an elliptical arc rotated at any angle.
Fixed Ratio	Draw an elliptical arc with the axis set at a fixed ratio.

When faced with so many choices, the beginner's obvious question is "Which one should I use?" There are some clues available in the names of the various tools. Three arc tools are reserved for creating ellipses, three more are limited to situations requiring tangency. These situations will be dealt with in separate sections as the chapter continues. That leaves five tools for general-purpose drafting of arcs.

Work through the following exercise before reading the guidelines for placement later in the chapter. Draw three regular polygons, and try to place an arc along each as indicated. Use the information in the status bar to help you *attempt* to place each arc. You may not be successful each time. Doing this will help you understand how arc commands work, and better able to appreciate the arc-placement guidelines to follow.

NOTE: *Arcs are always drawn in a counterclockwise direction in TurboCAD.*

Place an Arc Along a Regular Polygon

1. Start TurboCAD. Select the Normal template and click OK.
2. Adjust the screen grid (Menu: Tools|Grid and the Advance Grid tab) to Spacing of .125, Divisions of 4, and Frequency of 1 for both X and Y.
3. Click and hold on the Line tool until the flyout toolbar appears. Select Polygon.

Polygon tool

4. Select Snap to Grid from the Snaps toolbar, left side of the screen.
5. Toward the left side of the sheet, click on the intersection of two major grid lines. Move the cursor up to the next major grid line (1") and click again to finish the regular polygon.

6. Repeat the process two more times to the right, creating three identical regular polygons as illustrated.

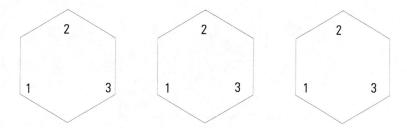

Three regular polygons in a line

7. Turn on the Vertex snap tool.
8. Select Arc Center and Radius from the arc flyout toolbar.

Arc center and radius tool

9. By following the prompts at the bottom of the screen, attempt to construct an arc on the first polygon that starts *exactly* at point 1, passes *precisely* through point 2 and ends *exactly* on point 3. Click on the grid at the center of the polygon to start the arc using this tool.

10. Select Double Point from the Arc flyout toolbar, and again attempt to place an arc that connects the same three points.

Double Point arc tool

11. Select Start/Included/End (1-2-3) from the Arc flyout toolbar, and attempt the same procedure on the third polygon.

Start/Included/End arc (1-2-3) tool

If all went well, two of the commands were able to draw the specified arc. Arc Center and Radius, and Start/Included/End both worked, but Double Point didn't come close.

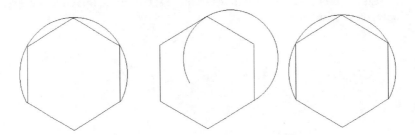

Attempts to place arcs on three regular polygons

Each arc command is designed for specific situations. There is some overlap in their capabilities, but sometimes there is only one tool that makes sense. Here are some guidelines:

- If you know the exact midpoint of the arc (the point midway along the length of the arc, not the center of the radius), use Start/Included/End.
- If you know the center point (radius) and the start of the arc, use Arc Center and Radius.
- If you know the start, end and center of the arc, use Arc Center and Radius.
- If you don't know the radius of the arc, use Start/Included/End.
- If you need to create two or more arcs that share a common center point, use Concentric.

Arc Placement Techniques

Each arc tool has a standard placement technique. Follow the instructions below to practice using each arc tool as part of completing a geometric construction project. Before each project is a general description of the tool's use. Be sure to erase each previous drawing before starting the next project.

 TIP: *Remember, 0 degrees on a circle is the equivalent of 3 o'clock; 90 degrees is 12 o'clock; 180 degrees is 9 o'clock; 270 degrees is 6 o'clock.*

Arc Center and Radius

Use Arc Center and Radius tool to create an arc by defining its center, a point on its circumference, and the two end points (starting and ending angles of the arc). The construction problem is to create a wave pattern using arcs inside a circle.

First construction problem, waves in a circle

1. Make sure Snap Grid is on. Use Zoom Window (View toolbar, right side of screen) to get a close-up of one quadrant of the paper.
2. Click and hold on the circle tool until the flyout toolbar appears. Select Circle Center and Point.

Circle Center and Point tool

3. Move the cursor to a major grid intersection. Click to set the center of a circle.
4. Move the cursor orthogonally two major grid lines, to set a radius of 1". Click to finish the circle.
5. Select the Arc Center and Radius tool from the Arc flyout toolbar.

Arc center and radius tool

6. The prompt line reads "Define the center point of the arc ..."
7. From the location at 180 degrees (9 o'clock) on the circle, move the cursor two minor grid lines right (1/4"). Click to set the center of an arc.
8. The prompt line reads "Define a second point on the arc ..."
9. Move the cursor right two minor grid lines (1/4") and click.
10. Click again in the same location to "Define the start angle of the arc." (The first end point of the arc.)
11. Move the cursor straight left to the location at 180 degrees (9 o'clock) on the circle, and click to "Define the end angle of the arc."

First arc placed inside circle

12. The arc command is still active.

13. Click on the right end point of the first arc to set the center of the next arc.

14. Move the cursor right 1/2" (4 minor grid lines) and click to "Define a second point on the arc."

15. Click at the same location a second time to "Define the start angle of the arc."

16. Move the cursor to the left end point of the first arc and click to finish.

Two arcs inside circle

17. The arc command is still active.

18. Click on the grid intersection halfway between the right endpoints of the first two arcs.

19. Move the cursor right 6 grid lines (3/4") and click to set the radius of the new arc.

20. Click again at the same location to start the arc.

21. Move the cursor to the common left endpoints of the first two arcs and click to finish.

Three arcs inside circle

22. Click on the Select tool, and select the three arcs. This is easily done with one selection rectangle if "Open Window Mode" is off in the local menu. Or, you may select the arcs with Menu: Edit|Select By|Entity Type and choose Arc.

23. From the menu, select Edit|Copy Entities|Radial.

24. Click on the right endpoint of the second arc (which is also the center point of the circle) to define the center of the radial copy process.

25. The prompt says "Define the step angle."

26. Press <Tab> repeatedly until the value in Sets is highlighted in the Edit Bar. Type 2.

27. Press <Tab> once to highlight the value in Angle. Type 180 and press <Enter>.

28. Click anywhere on screen to deselect the arcs.

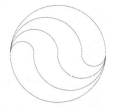

Arcs copied using Radial copy

Concentric Arc

Use the Concentric Arc tool when you need to draw a series of arcs that share a common center point. Remember that arcs are always drawn counterclockwise in TurboCAD.

Third construction problem

1. Select the Single Line tool.
2. Using the intersection of two major grid lines as a center point, draw a symmetrical cross with each line extending 3/8" from the center.

Draw a symmetrical cross

3. In each quadrant formed by the lines of the cross, draw three lines each 3/8" long, as illustrated.

NOTE: *The Parallel Line tool or a copy tool could have been used in this part of the exercise, but the lines are so short and easy to draw with Snap to Grid that there is no time saved by switching to another tool.*

Draw three parallel lines in each quadrant

4. Select the Concentric Arc tool from the arc flyout toolbar.

5. The prompt reads "Define the center point of the arc ..."

6. Click on the right end point of the right line which formed the original cross, to choose it as the center point for the arcs to be drawn.

7. The prompt reads "Define a second point ..."

8. Move the cursor one grid line down and click to set a point on the arc's circumference.

9. The prompt reads "Define the start angle of the arc ..."

10. Click at the same location used to set the circumference.

11. Move the cursor straight up to draw an arc that ends on the line directly above the center point of the arc.

Use Concentric Arc to draw first arc

12. The Concentric Arc tool is still active, and will use the center previously defined to draw other arcs.

13. The prompt reads "Define a second point on the arc ..." Move the cursor 1/8" (one grid line) below the start of the first arc. Click twice. The first click will set the radius of the arc; the second click will start the arc.

14. Move the cursor 1/8" above the top end of the first arc, and click to set a second arc.

15. Move the cursor 1/8" below the start of the second arc and click twice.

16. Move the cursor 1/8" above the top end of the second arc and click to finish a third arc.

Draw two more arcs

17. Click on the Select tool and select the three arcs.

18. From the Menu, select Edit|Copy Entities|Radial.

19. The prompt reads "Define the center of the copy process." Click at the center of the original cross.

20. Press the <Tab> key until Sets is highlighted in the Edit Bar. Type 4.

21. Press the <Tab> key to highlight Angle. Type 90, and press <Enter>.

Use Copy Radial to finish the drawing

Double Point Arc

The Double Point Arc tool lets you draw an arc by defining the endpoints of its diameter.

Third construction problem

1. Make sure Snap to Grid is on.

2. Select the Concentric Circle tool from the circle flyout toolbar.

3. Move the cursor to the intersection of two major grid lines and click to set the center of a circle.

4. Move left one minor grid line (1/8") and click to finish a circle.

5. Move left one minor grid line (1/8") and click to finish a second circle.

6. The circle tool is still active.

7. Move left to the second major grid line and click to create a third circle.

8. Click the Select tool.

9. Click on the Double Point Arc tool from the arc flyout toolbar.

Start by drawing three circles using the same center point

10. Move the cursor to the location at 180 degrees (9 o'clock) on the larger of the two interior circles. Click to start an arc.

11. The prompt reads "Define a second point..." Move the cursor to the location at 0 degrees (3 o'clock) on the largest circle and click to set the angle of the arc.

12. "Define the start angle of the arc." Click again at the same location.

13. The prompt reads "Define the end angle of the arc." Move the cursor right to the location at 180 degrees (9 o'clock) on the larger interior circle and click to finish the arc.

An arc has been added to the circles

14. Click on the Select tool and select the arc.

15. From the menu, select Edit|Copy Entities|Fit Radial Copy.

16. Click on the center of the three circles to "Define the center of the copy process."

17. Press <Tab> repeatedly until the value in Sets is highlighted in the Edit Bar. Type 8.

18. Press <Tab> to highlight Angle in the Edit Bar. Type 360 and press <Enter>.

19. Click anywhere in the drawing area to deselect the original arc.

Use Fit Radial Copy to complete the construction problem

Start/Included/End (1-2-3) Arc

Third construction problem

1. Make sure Snap to Grid is active.
2. Select the Concentric Circle tool from the circle flyout toolbar.
3. Move the cursor to the intersection of two major grid lines and click to set the center of a circle.
4. Move left two minor grid lines (1/4") and click to finish the circle.
5. Move left two major grid lines (1") and click to finish a second circle.

Start third construction problem by drawing two circles

6. Select Start/Included/End (1-2-3) from the arc flyout toolbar.

Start/Included/End (1-2-3) arc tool

7. Move the cursor to the location at 180 degrees on the larger circle. Click to start the arc.
8. "Define the middle point of the arc." Locate the grid intersection four lines down from the top of the circle (90 degrees or 12 o'clock) and click to set the second point of the arc.

9. "Define the end point of the arc." Move the cursor to the location at 0 degrees (3 o'clock) on the larger circle and click to finish the arc.

An arc has been added to the circles

10. Select the arc.

11. From the menu, select Edit|Copy Entities|Mirror.

12. "Define the first point of the mirror." Move the cursor to the location at 180 degrees (9 o'clock) on the larger circle and click to start the mirror axis line.

13. Move the cursor right to the location at 0 degrees (3 o'clock) and click to finish the mirror, copying the arc.

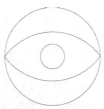

Use Copy Entities|Mirror to copy the arc

14. Select both arcs.

15. From the menu, select Edit|Copy Entities|Fit Radial Copy.

16. Click on the center of the circle to set the center for the copying.

17. Press <Tab> until Sets is highlighted in the Edit Bar. Type 4.

18. Press <Tab> to highlight Angle in the Edit Bar. Type 360 and press <Enter>.

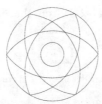

Fit Radial Copy is used to finish the construction problem

Drawing Arcs with the Edit Bar

Snaps and mouse entry were used to draw all the arcs so far. It is also possible to use the Edit Bar in various combinations with the mouse to draw arcs. To do so requires using the Lock feature of the Edit bar. The small boxes to the left of the Radius and Circumf. fields are the Lock boxes. If a value is entered in one of the fields, and you activate the lock for that field (by clicking on the box—an X appears), that value is set even if you move the cursor on screen. If you know specific values for the arc you need to draw, such as the radius, the circumference, or a starting or ending angle, you can enter the appropriate value in the Edit Bar as part of drawing the arc. To avoid moving the mouse unnecessarily, press the <Tab> key to engage the Edit Bar. Each press of the <Tab> key moves one step through the Edit Bar fields. In the illustration below, the Edit Bar has been moved into the drawing area, and a 2" radius has been specified by typing "2 in." in the Radius field and clicking the Lock Box. When the Edit Bar is floating in the drawing area, the name of the command being used appears as the title of the box instead of "Edit Bar."

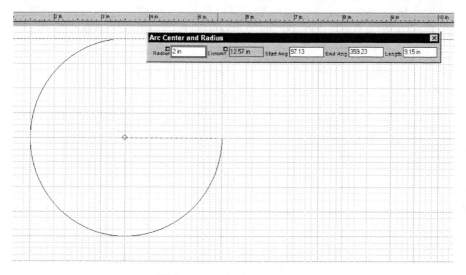

Edit bar settings for drawing a 2" arc

Drawing Tangent Arcs, Lines and Circles

Lines, arcs and circles may all be drawn tangent to arcs and circles. To draw a entity tangent to an arc or circle is to draw it so that the lines of the two objects come into contact but do not intersect. The two tools used to draw arcs tangent to other objects have already been listed. The other tangent tools are:

Tool	Action
Circle Tangent to Arc	Draw a circle tangent to another circle or arc.
Circle Tangent to Line	Draw a circle tangent to a line.
Tangent Arc Point	Draw a line tangent to an arc or circle, touching the arc at the line's midpoint.
Tangent To Arc	Draw a line tangent to an arc or circle, with the line's second end point touching the arc.
Tangent From Arc	Draw a line tangent to an arc, with the line's first endpoint touching the arc.
Tangent to 2 Arcs	Draw a line tangent to two arcs, with each endpoint of the line touching one of the arcs.

Complete the following construction problem to gain experience with some of the tangent commands available in TurboCAD. The completed diagram is a cam assembly, a typical mechanical engineering drawing. For this exercise you will shut off the screen grid and use a variety of snap commands.

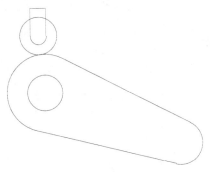

Next construction problem, cam assembly

1. Click on No Snap in the Snaps Toolbar.

2. From the menu, select Tools|Grid and click the "Show Grid" box to shut off the grid. Click OK.

3. Select Circle Center and Point from the Circle flyout toolbar.

4. Click anywhere on the paper to start a circle.

5. Press <Tab> and type .295 for radius. Press <Enter>.

6. The circle command is still active. Right-click to summon the local menu. Click on local snap and select Arc Center.

7. Click on the circle.

8. Press <Tab> and type .64 for radius. Press <Enter>.

First two circles drawn using the Edit Bar

9. Select the Line tool.

10. Right-click to access the local menu. Click on local snap and select Arc Center. Click on the larger circle.

11. Press <Tab>, type 2.45 for length; press <Tab>, type 340 (for angle) <Enter>.

12. Select the Circle Center and Point tool.

13. Right-click, local snap, Vertex.

14. Click on the right end of the line.

15. Press <Tab>, type .36 for radius. Press <Enter>.

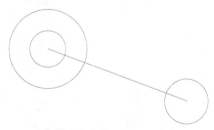

A third circle has been placed

16. Click on Tangent to 2 Arcs in the Line flyout toolbar.

17. The prompt reads "Pick an arc." Click on the top side of the larger left circle.

18. "Choose the tangent." Click on the top side of the circle on the right.

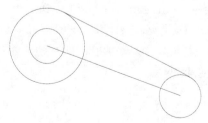

The second line is tangent to two circles

19. The Tangent to 2 Arcs command is still active.

20. Click on the bottom side of the larger left circle.

21. Click on the bottom side of the circle on the right.

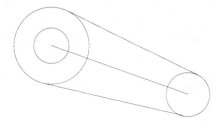

A second tangent line is added to the bottom

22. Click on the Line tool.

23. Select Vertex Snap from the Snap toolbar.

24. Click on the left endpoint of the bottom tangent line.

25. Click on the left endpoint of the top tangent line.

26. Repeat the process for the circle on the right side of the diagram.

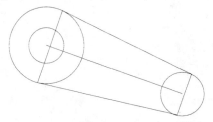

Lines connect the ends of the tangent lines

27. Click on the Select tool.

28. From the menu, select Modify|Object Trim.

29. Click on the left (nearly vertical) line to select it as the cutting edge.

30. Move the cursor right and click on the larger circle.

31. Press <Esc> to deselect the cutting edge. The Object Trim tool is still active.

32. Click on the right (nearly vertical) line to select it as the cutting edge.

33. Move the cursor a little to the left and click on the circle.

34. Click on the Select tool.

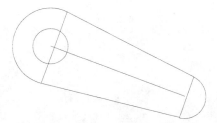

Object Trim was used to remove a half circle from each side

35. Use the Select tool and the <Delete> key to delete the two cutting edges and the line running through the center of the diagram.

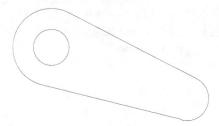

Three interior straight lines removed

36. Select the Tangent to Arc tool from the Circle flyout toolbar.

37. Click on the top of the largest arc, left side of the diagram.

38. Press <Tab> and set the Radius as .31. Press <Enter>.

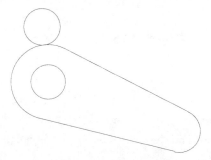

The new circle is tangent to the left side of the existing arc

39. Click on Snap Arc Center in the Snaps toolbar.

40. Select Circle Center and Point from the Circle flyout toolbar.

41. Click on the last circle placed.

42. Press <Tab>, type .14, press <Enter>.

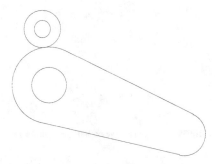

A new circle, placed inside the previous one

43. Click on Quadrant Snap in the Snaps toolbar. Deselect any other active snap.

44. Select the Line tool. Click on the larger of the two upper circles at 180 degrees (9 o'clock) and at 0 degrees (3 o'clock).

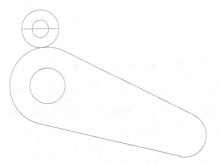

Use Quadrant Snap to add the new line

45. Click on the intersection of the left bisecting line and the small circle.

46. Click on Ortho Mode in the Snaps toolbar. All other snaps will be shut off.

47. Move the cursor straight up. Press <Tab>, type .45 <Enter>.

48. Repeat the process on the right side (Quadrant Snap, start line, Ortho mode, set distance).

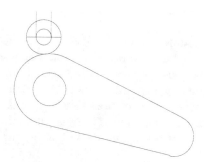

Use Quadrant Snap and Ortho Mode to draw two new lines

49. Click on the Select tool.
50. From the menu select Modify|Object Trim.
51. Click on the line bisecting the top circle as the cutting edge.
52. Click on the top side of the inner circle.

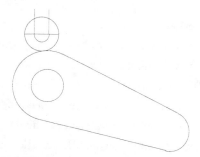

Use Object Trim to remove the top of the upper inner circle

53. Click on the Select tool.
54. Select and delete the bisecting line used as the cutting edge.
55. Select the Line tool and the Vertex Snap.
56. Click on the endpoints of the two lines extending vertically, to close the gap.

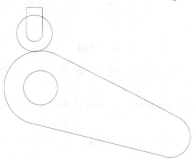

Close the gap on top with a single line

Using Ellipses

The ellipse is a common feature in both architectural and engineering applications. TurboCAD offers six elliptical tools, three for complete ellipses, and three for elliptical arcs. To draw a true ellipse on paper, you need a string tied at the ends to form a loop, and two pins. Stick the two pins into the paper and lay the loop around them. Draw with the pencil, using the string as a guide. Keep the string taut, so that every point on the line you draw is the same distance from both pins. The finished product is an ellipse. The definition of an ellipse is "the path of a point that moves so that the sum of its distances from two fixed points is constant."

The various ellipse tools define a bounding rectangle. The length and width of the rectangle correspond to the length and width of the ellipse. If you know the length values for the two axis that define the ellipse, type them in the Edit Bar.

When you need to be exact, placing an ellipse correctly is much easier if you draw lines or place points beforehand, then snap to these locations to place the axis points of the ellipse. Or, snap to existing objects in the drawing.

Tool	Action
Elliptical Arc	Draw an elliptical arc by defining its bounding rectangle.
Rotated Elliptical Arc	Draw an elliptical arc rotated at any angle.
Fixed Ratio El. Arc	Draw an elliptical arc by defining a ratio and identifying either axis.
Ellipse	Draw an ellipse by defining its bounding rectangle.
Rotated Ellipse	Draw an ellipse rotated at any angle.
Fixed Ratio Ellipse	Draw an ellipse by defining a ratio and identifying either axis.

Draw a Standard Ellipse

1. Activate the Ellipse tool from the circle flyout toolbar.

Ellipse tool

2. Define the first point or corner of the bounding rectangle, then do one of the following:

   • Move the cursor and click to define the diagonally opposed corner of the bounding rectangle;

   • Specify the lengths of the ellipse's major and minor axes in the Edit Bar, then press <Enter>.

Draw a Rotated Ellipse

1. Activate the Rotated Ellipse tool from the circle flyout toolbar.

Rotated ellipse tool

2. Click to define the center point of the ellipse.

3. Click to define a point, specifying an angle and distance from the center point. This creates an axis from the defined point, through the center point, to an opposite point the same distance from the center point. You can view this axis on the screen as you adjust the position of the point using the mouse or Coordinate Fields.

4. Define a second point to specify the length of the opposite axis. This axis will be perpendicular to the first axis.

Alternatively, you can define the center point of the ellipse, specify the length and angle of the major axis and the length of the minor axis in the Edit Bar, then press <Enter>.

Draw an Elliptical Arc

The lengths of the major and minor axis of the elliptical arc are determined by the lengths of the sides of the bounding rectangle. The axes of the arc will be orthogonal; however, you can rotate the arc after you have created it using the editing tools.

1. Activate the Elliptical Arc tool from the arc flyout toolbar.

Elliptical arc tool

2. Define a point for the first corner of the bounding rectangle.

3. Define a point for the diagonally opposite corner of the bounding rectangle. TurboCAD draws an ellipse bounded by the rectangle that you have defined. A dotted line appears, extending from the center point of the ellipse to the cursor.

4. Move the cursor to change the dotted line to the angle at which you want the arc to start, then click to set the arc's starting angle.

5. Move the cursor counterclockwise to draw the arc, then click the mouse button to define the ending angle.

Alternatively, you can define the starting point of the elliptical arc, then specify its major and minor axes and starting and ending angles in the Edit Bar. You can also combine use of the mouse and Edit Bar.

Draw an Elliptical Rotated Arc

1. Activate the Rotated Elliptical Arc tool in the Arc flyout toolbar.

Rotated elliptical tool

2. Define the center point of the arc.

3. Define a point to specify an angle and distance from the center point. This creates an axis from the defined point, through the center point, to an opposite point the same distance from the center point. This is the major axis of the elliptical arc.

4. Define a third point to specify the length of the minor axis (perpendicular to the major axis). TurboCAD draws an ellipse with the specified major and minor axes. A dotted line appears, extending from the center point of the ellipse to the cursor.

5. Move the cursor to change the dotted line to the angle at which you want the arc to start, then click to set the arc's starting angle.

6. Move the cursor counterclockwise to draw the arc, then click the mouse button to define the ending angle.

Curve Tools

TurboCAD offers three curve tools, each with special properties.

The Spline is a continuous curve that connects from point to point as placed in the drawing. The Spline in manual drafting is a long, flat pliable strip of wood, metal or plastic used to draw curves. The advantage of the spline in manual drafting (and which carries over in the technology of the Spline command in TurboCAD) is that by tracing along the spline the curve is created as one continuous line, not a series of curved segments with awkward changes of direction connecting each curve. The final product is a smooth, continuous curve, not a series of fitted arcs or clipped circles.

While the Spline curve is best for smooth, regular curved lines, the Bezier curve tool is better for drawing irregularly shaped curved lines. Bezier curves are named for French engineer Pierre Bezier, who developed a curve-generation algorithm for car designers at Renault. Bezier curves have become standard in CAD programs in recent years because they are fast and the procedures used in drawing them become fairly predictable after one works with them for a while.

Bezier curves are defined by a set of control points, intermediate points placed in the drawing in addition to the curve and the points that define the position of the curved line. The control points act as magnets, affecting the shape of the curve depending on their location.

The Sketch tool is used for freehand drawing. Whether the lines drawn are elegant or ugly is completely up to the artist.

Tool	Action
Spline	Draw a continuous curve that connects a series of points.
Bezier	Draw a curve that connects two endpoints; the curve gravitates toward control points along its path.
Sketch	Freehand multiline drawn with mouse.

Curve Properties

Curves have special properties that can be set in the Curve property sheet of the Properties dialog. This property sheet lets you show or hide the frame of a Bezier or Spline curve, transform a Bezier curve into a Spline curve or vice versa. You can access the properties of a curve by double-clicking on it with the Select tool, or by selecting the curve and then choosing Menu: Format|Properties. The properties for curves are accessed via right-clicking the curve's button on the toolbar.

To close a Bezier or Spline curve, right-click on the local menu and select Close. To end either curve without forming a closed loop, right-click on the local menu and select Finish.

Using Curves to Create Parabolas and Spirals

Certain curves have special properties in engineering, architecture and in nature. The parabola, for example, defines a comet's path around the sun, and is used to design reflecting surfaces, road sections and arches. The spiral is found throughout nature in such things as DNA, the chambered nautilus, the abalone, the spider web, and the shape of some galaxies.

Follow the steps below to construct a parabola and a logarithmic spiral. Both objects require that you draw construction aids to identify points along each curve. Instead of detailed steps, the instructions for these two exercises give you guidelines to follow, along with illustrations showing the details.

Construct a Parabola

1. Using Snap to Grid, construct a rectangle four units wide and eight units deep. Use Points to mark the units along the top, left and bottom as illustrated.

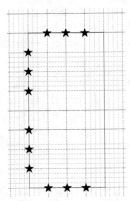

Use the grid to construct a rectangle and place points

2. Use straight lines to connect the points along the top and the bottom with the midpoint of the right side of the rectangle. Draw straight lines from the points along the right side, forming intersections as illustrated.

3. Use the Bezier curve to draw a shape connecting the points as identified. Shut off Grid Snap, and select Intersection Snap from the Snap Toolbar. To finish the curve, right-click and select Finish from the local menu. The finished shape is a parabola.

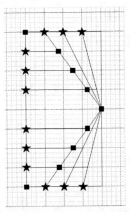

Construction lines added to rectangle; squares mark points to place curve

4. Erase the construction aids.

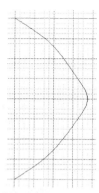

Parabola after all construction aids removed

Construct a Logarithmic Spiral

1. From the menu, select Tools|Grid. Change the grid type to Polar. Set Angular to 15 and Radial to .125 in.

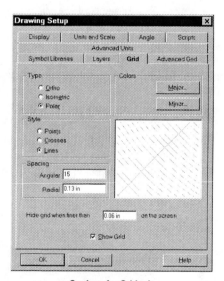

Settings for Grid tab

2. Click the Advanced Grid tab. Set the origin for both X and Y to 5 in.; set the Divisions for both Minor A and Minor R to 1. Click OK.

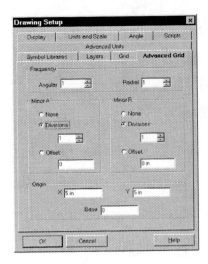

Settings for the Advanced Grid tab

3. Click on Snap to Grid in the Snaps toolbar. Select the Spline curve from the Curve flyout toolbar.

4. Use Zoom Window to get a close-up view of the center section of the polar grid. Click on the center point to start the spiral. Move the cursor up along the Angle Grid line pointing straight up (12 'clock or 90 degrees) until you reach the first intersection with a Radial grid line. Then move along the first Radial grid line until you intersect the next Angular grid line. Click to set a point on the spiral. Continue to set point using this one-out, one-over pattern. Use the scroll bars and/or the zoom commands to adjust the view as you place the curve. To finish, right-click and select Finish from the local menu.

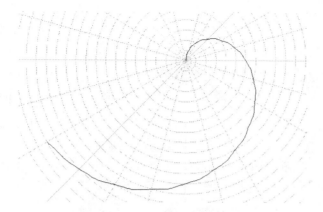

The first few segments of a spiral

Node Editing

TurboCAD offers a special set of editing capabilities for entities called Node Edit mode. In Node Edit mode you can reshape entities by directly manipulating particular points called *nodes*.

- Add, delete, and move nodes on entities composed of line segments (including lines, double lines, polygons).
- Divide line segments into any number of subsegments of equal length.
- Break polygons, making them into multilines.
- Close multilines, making them into polygons.
- Close the endpoints of double lines.
- Reshape Bezier and spline curves by adding, deleting, and moving nodes on the line segments that form the curve's frame.
- Change the radius of circles and circular arcs.
- Change the major and minor axes of ellipses and elliptical arcs.
- Change the start and end angles of circles, ellipses, and arcs.
- Close arcs, making them into circles.
- Divide circles, arcs, and ellipses into arc segments of equal angular length.

To activate Node Edit mode, first select the entity that you wish to edit, then click the right mouse button in the drawing area to display the local menu. From the local menu, select Node Edit. The appearance of the selection will change. Instead of a selection box with handles, you will see highlighted objects with nodes displayed as blue rectangles. The number and placement of the nodes depends on the type of object selected.

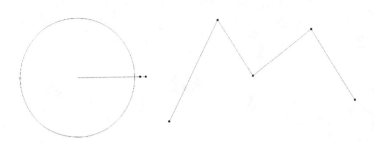

Selected objects in Node Edit mode

You can only edit one entity at a time in Node Edit mode. You cannot use this mode to work with multiple selected entities or groups. To edit the nodes of an entity that is in a group, first select the group, then break it into its component entities using the Menu: Format|Explode command. If the entity is part of a nested group, you may have to use Explode more than once.

On Your Own

Experiment with Node Edit on your own. Draw a variety of entities, then use Node Edit on each entity to reshape or break entities. If you have not already encountered the other exercises in this book that use Node Edit, refer to the Index to find them.

To delete a node, select the entity and enter Node Edit mode. Hold down the <Ctrl> key while placing the mouse cursor over the node you wish to delete. When you are in the correct position, the cursor will change to an icon showing a node being thrown into a trash can. Click to delete the node. If you delete a node on a rectangle, for example, it immediately becomes a triangle. It is not possible to use node delete to remove a node from a single line segment or to convert a polygon to a single line.

11

Dimensioning

Placing Exact Measurements

As explained in Chapter Eight, text in a CAD drawing bridges the worlds of verbal and visual expression. Labeling a TurboCAD drawing gives the "reader" a frame of reference to help interpret drawings.

Often CAD drawings are created only to express a design idea, so informally labeling parts of the drawing is enough. But many CAD drawings are used as the primary construction plans. These drawings need more than simple labels. Whoever uses the drawing needs to know the exact dimensions of objects in the drawing.

TurboCAD supports automatic dimensioning, a series of commands that let you measure the distance between two points, draw reference lines, measure lengths and angles, and print measurements on the drawing near the measured objects. By *dimensioning*, we refer to the act of placing the measurements or other important information about an object into the drawing.

By default, dimensions in TurboCAD are associative. This means that if a dimensioned object changes in size, the dimensioning already on the screen will automatically update to accurately display the new length, angle, etc. If you don't want associativity to automatically update dimensions, this feature can be turned off in the Dimensioning Property Sheet. To check if a dimension line is associated with an entity, select the entity. Any dimensions associated with it will be colored blue.

Using dimensions in your designs makes the drawings easy to interpret. But the process of placing dimensions in a drawing can be confusing to the new user because of the large number of variations available in the dimensioning commands. But once you know a few rules of thumb, the number of decisions quickly dwindle down. This chapter will provide reference material on dimensions, exercises to guide you through using dimensions for the first time, and will offer a few guidelines for knowing when and how to place dimensions in your drawings.

Elements of Dimensioning

When TurboCAD dimensions an object, it calculates the object's length, angle, diameter, or radius (as requested), draws two lines to show the distance, draws a line or arc with arrows on each end between these two lines, and displays the measurement. These pieces can be divided into three basic components:

- The dimension lines, with arrows pointing to either end of the dimension.
- Extension lines, which connect the dimension line to the object being measured.
- Dimension text, normally displaying the distance being measured in World units.

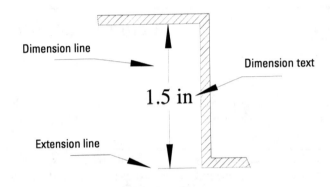

Parts of a dimension

Extension lines have optional line segments that continue the extension outward beyond the dimension line (extensions to the extension). Extension lines are also called witness lines by some professions.

A dimension can have interior dimension lines, as shown in the preceding figure, or two exterior dimension lines. Exterior dimension lines can be supplemented with an optional interior line.

Format Property Sheets

Three Format Property Sheets control the shape of dimension arrows and the position of text relative to the dimension line. You can summon the dimension format property sheets in one of two ways: Either Right-Click the dimension tool on the Insert Entity toolbar; or, if the dimension tool is active, select Menu: Format|Properties.

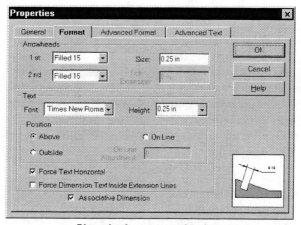

Dimension format properties sheet

Dimension Format Property Sheet

The Format Properties sheet provides controls for basic dimensioning features, including the shape of arrowheads, the size and appearance of text, and the positioning of dimensioning lines.

Arrowheads

1st and 2nd. Click in these drop-down boxes to choose dimension arrow shapes. The arrowheads can have angles of 15, 30 or 45 degrees; they can be filled, open, or closed. If you like, you can choose None (no arrowhead at all), Tick (a simple angled line), Hollow Dot or Solid Dot.

Size. Click the Size field to choose a size for the length of the arrowhead, or type in a custom size. (How to determine the correct size for an arrowhead is discussed later in the chapter.)

Tick Extension. If you set the arrowhead to Tick in the 1st and 2nd boxes, use this field to specify the length of each tick's extension line.

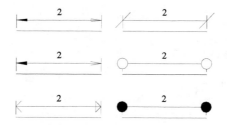

Dimension arrow shapes

Text Position

Font. Use the Font text box to choose a TrueType font for the dimension text. All TrueType fonts installed on your computer will be available.

Height. Click this text box to choose a text height, or type in a custom height. You can set the height in either World or Paper units, to match your current working mode.

Position. Choose Outside if you want the text placed outside of the dimension line; choose Above if you want the text "above" the dimension line ("above" is relative to the orientation of the text, not relative to your screen); or choose On Line if you want to place the text directly on the dimension line. The position can be manually adjusted (see the next control).

On Line Adjustment. Type a number into this text box to specify the distance of the text above or below the dimension line. A value of zero (the default value) will place the text on the same level as the dimension line. Higher values move the text above the line ("above" is relative to the orientation of the text); lower (negative) values move the text below the line.

Force Text Horizontal. Check this box if you want the dimension text to be horizontal no matter how the dimension is rotated.

Force Dimension Text Inside Extension Lines. Click this box if you want to keep dimension text between the extension lines, regardless of the distance between the extension lines. If you leave this box unchecked, TurboCAD will decide whether to place dimension text inside or outside the extension lines.

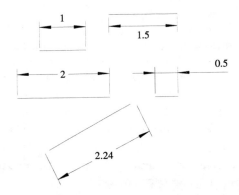

Various positions for dimension text

Advanced Format Property Sheet

The Advanced Format Property Sheet controls a variety of more specialized options for the positioning of dimension lines. If you are overwhelmed by the number of options and details available, you can bypass this property sheet and the next one (Advanced Text) until you are more comfortable with basic dimensioning operations.

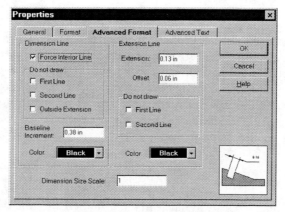

Advanced Format Property Sheet

Dimension Lines

Force Interior Line: Sometimes you will dimension an object so small that TurboCAD must place the text outside the extension lines. Check this box if you want such dimension lines to still have a line running between the extension lines. If unchecked, TurboCAD will only draw an interior dimension line if the text fits between the two extensions.

Do Not Draw: This set of check boxes lets you choose whether or not to draw the first, second, and outside extension lines. (Check the view in the preview box to see each effect.) To check one of these boxes is to say that you don't want the object to appear.

Baseline Increment: If you are creating baseline dimensions (also know as continuous dimensions), you may control the distance between each dimension here.

Color: This box modified only the color of the dimension line. Extension lines and dimension text have their own settings boxes.

Extension Lines

Extension lines are the small lines that extend out from dimension arrows. They link a dimension with the object being measured. This section of the Advanced Format Property Sheet controls the appearance of these lines. The upcoming section of this chapter entitled The Secret to Simple Dimension Formats provides ideas on using these controls.

Extension: The number in this box is the length of each extension line. Refer to the guidelines later in this chapter for advice on setting this length.

Offset: Offset is the gap between an extension line and the object being measured. If you want the extension line to abut the object being measured, set this value to zero. Otherwise, use the guidelines later in this chapter to set this value.

Do Not Draw: As with dimension lines, you have the choice of independently setting the appearance of extension lines in the drawing.

Color: You may set extension lines to any available color.

Dimension Size Scale

In a large and detailed drawing, you may want some dimensions to stand out more than others. The best way to do this is to use two sizes of dimension lines. But changing all the settings that control the size of a dimension line would be a tedious task. Instead, use the Dimension Size Scale text box to set the scale size of dimensions. For your most important dimensions lines, set this value to 1. For other dimensions, set this value to something smaller, like .75, which would cause subsequent dimensions to be place at 75% of the sizes listed in the various dimension settings.

Dimensioning Tools

Eleven dimensioning tools are available in the flyout toolbar from the Insert Entity toolbar, or from the menu (Insert|Dimension|*tool*). The tools, and their actions, are:

Tool	Action
Horizontal Dimension	Measure and display the horizontal distance between two points or the horizontal length of a specific object.
Vertical Dimension	Measure and display the vertical distance between two points or the vertical length of a specific object.
Parallel Dimension	Measure and display the absolute distance between two points or the absolute distance of a specific object.
Rotated Dimension	Measure and display the absolute distance of an object, but rotate the display to the same angle as the object being measured.
Datum Dimension	Display a progression of measurements connected to angled leader lines, generally along a horizontal or vertical axis.
Baseline Dimension	Display a progression of parallel measurements that share a common baseline (starting point).
Continuous Dimension	Display a progression of parallel measurements, each new measurement starting where the previous measurement ended.
Angular Dimension	Measure the angle formed by two lines, by points on the perimeter of a circle or arc, or the angle formed by any two points relative to a defined vertex.
Radius Dimension	Measure and display the radius of an arc or circle.
Diameter Dimension	Measure and display the diameter of an arc or circle.
Leader Dimension	Draw an arrow and a line and add text as a label.

Linear Dimensioning Methods

The first seven dimension methods listed above are collectively known as linear dimensions. They measure distances along a line (real or imagined). But to understand how these methods differ, we need to consider only three for the moment: Horizontal, Vertical and Parallel Dimensioning . How these three measure lengths is very different one from the other.

Horizontal Dimension will display only the horizontal distance of an entity, or the horizontal distance between two points that you identify. If the object is not parallel to the horizon, the distance being measured is not the same as the actual length of the object. Complete the following exercise to gain experience with this.

Practice Horizontal Dimensioning

1. Launch TurboCAD; accept the Normal template.
2. Use Snap to Grid and Irregular Polygon (in the Single Line flyout toolbar) to draw the eight-sided irregular polygon shown below. The exact length of each side is not crucial.

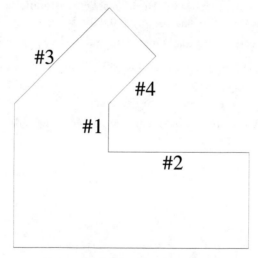

Draw an eight-sided polygon to start the exercise

3. Select the Horizontal Dimensioning tool from the Dimensioning flyout toolbar in the Entity Insert toolbar.

Horizontal dimensioning tool

4. Deselect Snap to Grid; select Vertex Snap.

5. Click on the upper end of line Number 1.

6. Click on the lower end of the same line.

7. Right-click for the local menu. Select Local Snap|No Snap.

8. Click anywhere to place the dimension line.

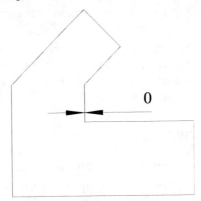

Horizontal dimension of a vertical distance

TurboCAD shows "0 in." because the Horizontal Dimensioning tool can only calculate horizontal distances. This line has no horizontal distance, it only has vertical distance.

Go ahead now and use Horizontal Dimensioning the way it was intended.

1. The Horizontal Dimensioning tool is still active. Click on the left endpoint of line Number 2.

2. Click on the right endpoint of the same line.

3. Right-click, and select Local Snap|No Snap. Move the dimension line where you please, and click to place it in the drawing.

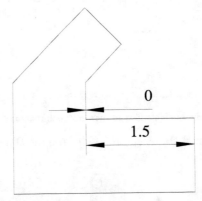

New dimension line also measures a horizontal distance

While there are times when a length to be dimensioned is either the horizontal or vertical run of an entity, more often the absolute length of an item is needed. The Parallel dimensioning tool will calculate and display the exact (absolute) length of an item no matter at what angle it sits in the drawing. For general purpose linear dimensioning, it is the tool to use first.

1. Select Parallel Dimensioning from the Dimensioning flyout toolbar.

Parallel dimensioning tool

2. Click on the upper endpoint of the polygon's top left line.
3. Click on the lower endpoint of the same line.
4. Right-click, and select Local Snap|No Snap. Move the dimension line where you please, and click to place it in the drawing.

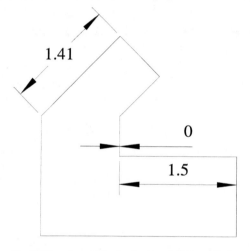

Top left line dimensioned using Parallel dimensioning

Rotated, Datum, Baseline and Continuous Dimensioning all work like Parallel — they measure an absolute linear distance, not a vertical or horizontal distance.

Manual, Segment and Entity Dimensioning

The linear dimensioning tools are equipped with three methods to locate entities and distances. The method used in the exercise above was manual dimensioning. You used a snap tool to locate endpoints, and you had to identify both ends of the entity before it could be dimensioned.

TurboCAD can automate the process of identifying entities for linear dimensioning. Segment dimensioning allows you to click once to associate the dimension with a line segment. Entity dimensioning allows you to click once to associate the dimension with an entire entity (such as a multiline, or a group). Segment and Entity are available as options in the local menu when a linear dimensioning command is active. Complete the exercise below to gain experience using both methods.

Segment Dimensioning

1. Change to the Select tool and delete the previous dimension lines.
2. Select Parallel Dimensioning.

Parallel Dimensioning tool button

3. Right-click and select Segment Dimensioning. Set snaps to No Snap using the Snap toolbar.
4. Click anywhere on line Number 4 and place the dimension line nearby. Click to finish.

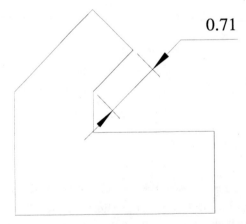

Parallel dimensioning using the Segment dimensioning option

Entity Dimensioning

1. The Parallel Dimensioning tool should still be active.
2. Right-click and select Entity Dimensioning (this will automatically deselect Segment Dimensioning).
3. Click anywhere on the same line (line Number 4) as selected just above.

4. Move the cursor up and to the left from the line. Notice the readout on the dimension line (even though it has not be placed in the drawing, the dimensioning text should be visible).

5. Now move the cursor down and to the right from the line. Notice how the readout changes.

6. Move the cursor down and to the right to the location you choose for the dimension line.

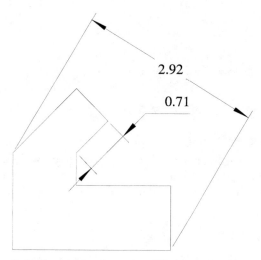

Entity dimensioning shows the width of the entire object

When Entity Dimensioning is active, selecting any individual line in a polygon or group only shows the tool at what angle it is dimensioning the entire object. As you moved the cursor around the screen before placing the dimension line, the angle changed, so the linear readout changed as well.

Used appropriately, Segment and Entity Dimensioning can make quick work of complex dimensioning jobs.

 Note: *When Segment or Entity Dimensioning is turned on, the dimensioning method stays active either until the other method is selected, or until you click on the name of the method in the local menu to deselect it.*

Angular Dimensioning

The Angular Dimensioning tool is used to measure angles. With it you can dimension:

- The angle formed by any two lines.
- The angle of an arc.
- The angle formed by any two points on the perimeter of a circle.
- A freeform angle that you create by defining a vertex node and two points.

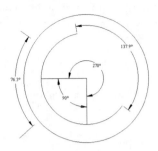

Angular dimensions

Follow the exercise below to gain experience using Angular Dimensioning.

Dimensioning an Angle Formed by Two Lines

1. Save or delete the existing drawing.
2. Use the Line tool, and any circle and arc tools to draw the entities shown below. The exact lengths and sizes are not crucial, but try to maintain the relationships between objects as illustrated.

Objects for next dimensioning exercise

3. Select the Angular Dimensioning tool from the Dimensioning flyout toolbar.

Angular dimensioning tool

4. Click anywhere along the upper line of the pair of lines that meet to form an angle.
5. Click anywhere along the lower line of the pair.

6. Move the cursor inside the angle, then outside. Notice how the dimension changes between measuring the inside angle and the outside angle.

7. Move the cursor inside the angle, select No Snap from the local menu, and place the dimension where you please.

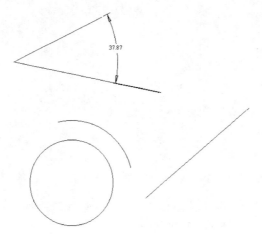

Dimensioning the angle of two lines

Dimensioning Angles on Circles

In the next exercise you will use other entities in the drawing to identify the portion of the circle to be dimensioned.

1. The Angular Dimension tool is still active.

2. Click anywhere on the circle. A rubberband line will appear, extending from the center of the circle to the mouse cursor.

3. The prompt line reads "Define first angle endpoint."

4. Select Snap Vertex from the Snaps menu.

5. Click where the two lines at the top of the drawing meet to form an angle.

6. The prompt now reads "Define second angle endpoint."

7. Move the cursor to the lower right portion of the screen and click on the lower endpoint of the single line.

8. Move the cursor inside the circle, then outside. Notice how the angular measurement changes as a result.

9. Select No Snap (from either the local menu or the Snaps toolbar), and place the dimension inside the circle.

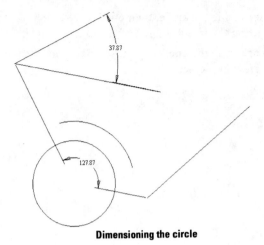

Dimensioning the circle

Dimensioning Angles on Arcs

1. The Angular Dimensioning tool is still active. Click on the arc located just above the circle. Adjust the snaps as necessary.

2. Move the cursor above and below the arc. Move the cursor all the way below the circle and watch the changes in the measurement.

3. Move the cursor above the arc and place the dimension.

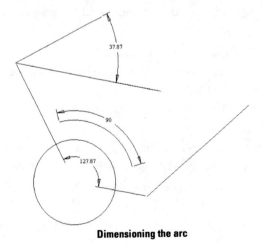

Dimensioning the arc

When you use the Angular Dimension tool on an arc, TurboCAD automatically dimensions the angle formed by the endpoints of the arc (the angle that would be formed by lines extending from the ends of the arc to the center). If you want to dimension the angle formed by any other two points on the perimeter of the arc, you can employ the Angle Node technique described in the next section, using snap modes to define points at the center and on the perimeter of the arc.

Dimensioning Freeform Angles

You can dimension the angle formed by any two points in the drawing space relative to a defined endpoint (vertex), using the Angle Node option in the local menu.

1. Select and delete each of the existing dimension lines. Be careful to leave the entities.
2. Select the Angular Dimensioning tool.
3. Right-click for local menu and select Angle Node.
4. Select Snap Vertex from the Snaps toolbar (if not already active).
5. Click on the upper endpoint of the single line, to identify it as the first of three points to define an angle.
6. The prompt reads "Define first angle endpoint."
7. Click on the lower end of the single line.
8. The prompt reads "Define second angle endpoint."
9. Click on the lower endpoint of the nearby arc.
10. Move the cursor above and below the single line, and notice how the dimension readout changes.
11. Place the dimension near the bottom of the single line by the arc, adjusting snaps as necessary.

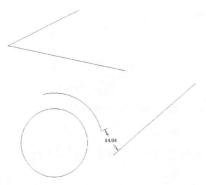

The angle framed by the line and the arc have been dimensioned

Radius and Diameter Dimensioning

The Radius and Diameter Dimensioning tools work on both arcs and circles. The technique for use is identical:

- Activate the tool.
- Click on the arc or circle.
- Click again to place the dimension.

Follow the steps below to practice using each tool.

Dimensioning the Radius of an Arc

1. Save your previous work and start a new drawing or delete all entities and dimension lines, to clear the screen.
2. Draw a circle and an arc, as illustrated below.

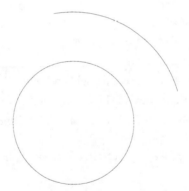

Arc and circle for Radial dimension exercise

3. Select the Radius Dimensioning tool from the Dimensioning flyout toolbar.

Radius dimensioning tool

4. Click No Snap in the Snaps toolbar, then click anywhere along the arc.
5. Move the cursor until the dimension line is in a position you like, then click to place the dimension.

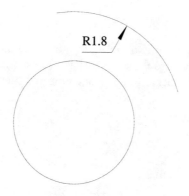

Radial dimension of arc

Dimension the Diameter of a Circle

1. Select Diameter Dimension from the Dimensioning flyout toolbar.

Diameter dimensioning tool

2. Click anywhere along the circumference of the circle.
3. Move the cursor until the dimension line is in a position you like, then click to place the dimension.

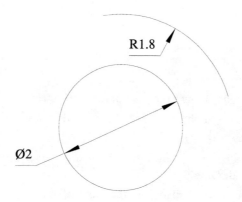

Diameter dimension placed on circle

Leader Dimensions

Use Leaders to place a note about an object into the drawing. Each Leader has an arrow and a line pointing from the note to the object. The Leader tool is similar to the Multiline tools in that it can contain an arbitrary number of connected line segments, oriented to any angle.

use this line

Leader dimension

The Leader has four parts:

- The arrow, which points to the object.
- The line, which can be more than one segment if necessary
- The shoulder, which serves as a base for the text.
- The text.

Follow the exercise below to become familiar with the Leader tool.

Label the Circle with a Leader

1. Select Leader from the Dimensioning flyout toolbar.

Leader tool

2. Make sure No Snap is active.
3. Click along the top edge of the circle.
4. The prompt reads "Define the next point of the string."
5. Press <Tab> to highlight the Text field in the Edit Toolbar.
6. Type "Circle #1"
7. Click to return control to the cursor. Move the cursor until you find a position you like for the leader line.
8. Right-click and select Finish from the local menu.

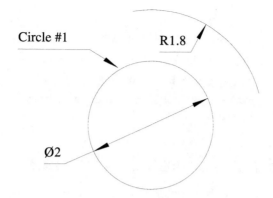

Leader used to label circle

In addition to placing the leader using the Finish command in the local menu, you can double-click in the drawing. A single-click causes a new section of the leader line to be drawn.

Professional Standards

Architecture and engineering, the two professions most commonly associated with drafting, have each developed guidelines for the appearance of drawings. If you need to have your drawings conform to either set of professional guidelines, you will have fewer decisions to make about dimension settings.

The guidelines that follow are generalizations on how professionals in these two fields practice dimensioning. There may well be alternative standards that are equally valid. If as part of your professional training you learned a method for dimensioning, use that as your standard. If you have no such background or training, you may want to consider the guidelines that follow for use in your work. To create your own template to reflect your particular standards, set up the dimensioning tools as you require in a blank file, then save the file as a template instead of a drawing.

Architectural drawings generally:

- Align dimensions to the object (TurboCAD tool: Parallel).
- Align dimension text to the object (Property Sheet: Force Text Horizontal Off).
- Have text placement above the dimension line (Property Sheet: Position|Above).
- Use tick marks, not arrows (Property Sheet: Arrowheads|1st and 2nd|Tick).
- Use closed arrow heads set at a 30-degree angle for leaders (Property Sheet: Arrowheads|1st and 2nd|Closed 30).

Engineering drawings generally:

- Place dimensions horizontally (TurboCAD tool: Horizontal).
- Place dimension text horizontal (Property Sheet: Force Text Horizontal On).
- Have text placement on the dimension line (Property Sheet: Position|On Line).
- Use closed arrow heads set at a 30-degree angle for both dimensions and leaders (Property Sheet: Arrowheads|1st and 2nd|Closed 30).

The Secret to Simple Dimension Formats

With so many variables available in formatting dimensions, how does one know the best style? The key is to eliminate the variables, and only make one decision. How? The secret is to set the size of the *drawing text* used for general labeling in a drawing. Surprised? It makes sense when you know the logic behind it.

In manual drafting there is a standard understanding of style which dictates dimension text should be smaller than text used to label parts of the drawing. The most common ratio is that dimension text is 75 percent as tall as regular text. If the text in a drawing is 1" tall, dimension text should be .75". Dimension text and the size of the arrowheads should be the same. So, once you know the size of label text in your drawing, you can quickly calculate the size of dimension text and arrowheads. If you regularly use the same size of text in your drawings, you can create a template to reflect this ratio. Incorporate it as part of your dimensions template, if you choose to make one.

The Seven Laws of Dimensioning

The beginning of this chapter mentioned that a few rules would be given to help you choose dimensioning variables. These guidelines will help you in designing how your dimensions should look, and how to use dimensions to their best advantage in your drawings.

I. Most CAD drawings don't require dimensioning. The primary purpose of most drawings is to convey a design idea. Only a few are used to actually carry out the design. The use of dimensions is a choice to be made, not an assumption to carry out.

II. Use professional standards if available and relevant. Following the conventional dimensioning standards established by architects, engineers, or other professionals who use drafting will eliminate the need to decide which of the many dimensioning variables to use.

III. Dimensioning lines should not be the focal point of a drawing. Dimensioning text should generally be 75 percent as tall as the average display text in a drawing.

IV. Put dimensioning lines on a layer by themselves and draw them in a color not otherwise used in the drawing.

V. If you are going to use the printed version of the drawing as an actual diagram for construction, set Force Text Horizontal Off (unless this conflicts with Rule II).

VI. If a drawing requires extensive dimensioning, and you are going to use it for construction, print the design in several parts instead of all on one sheet of paper.

VII. If you are going to print the drawing at a common scale (such as 1/4" = 1'), allow the scale of the drawing to speak for itself: State the scale in a legend box. To keep the drawing neat and readable, include only necessary dimensions. The user can measure others manually.

The Complete Guide to TurboCAD for Windows V3

12
Drawing Enrichment

Patterns, Color, and Linked Files

The drawings created so far have consisted of geometric entities, dimensions, and text. Using these elements you can create accurate and detailed drawings, but they probably won't win any awards. This chapter covers several TurboCAD features that can help bring life to your drawings. Some features provide visual enrichment and detailing, such as the use of hatch patterns, solid color fills, and drawings from other CAD programs. It is also possible to import graphic images created in non-CAD programs. You can also enhance your drawings by linking them to information files created with word processors, spreadsheets and other applications. It is even possible to add sound and video to your TurboCAD drawings, if your computer supports multimedia. In effect, TurboCAD can become a multimedia design presentation tool.

After these new features are introduced, there will be an exercise to help you become familiar with these capabilities. At the end of the chapter there will be a project that integrates several of the features introduced in this chapter, as well as commands and tools from earlier chapters.

Hatch Patterns and Solid Color Fills

Hatching is defined as the drawing of fine lines of repetitive detail. Hatch patterns are used for shading, to create a special design effect, or to identify an object as being made of a specific material. To hatch manually is a tedious time-consuming task, one that CAD virtually eliminates.

Forty hatch patterns ship with TurboCAD. As shown below, many of the hatches represent specific materials or elements commonly illustrated in various design professions. By name, the patterns are:

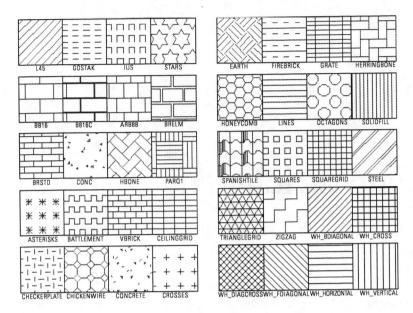

Forty hatch patterns available in TurboCAD

Solid color fills can also be placed in drawings. Use the *Brush* setting to place both hatch patterns and solid color fills. The Brush is not a separate tool, but a setting that affects existing drawing tools, similar to the way Pen sets the line style, width and color. The Brush property sheet is used to format the characteristics of both hatches and solid color fills.

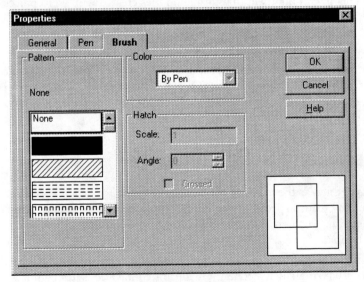

Brush property sheet

The Brush property sheet contains the following controls:

Pattern. Scroll through the Brush Style list box to select a hatch pattern. The name of the pattern is displayed just above the Brush Style list box.

Color. Click on the Color drop-down list box to select or change the color of a fill or hatch pattern. Choose the By Pen option if you want the Brush color to match the Pen color. Choose By Layer if you want the color to match the default color of the object's layer (set in the Layers property sheet).

Hatch. Scale, Angle, and the Crossed option are available in this section of the property sheet. Scale controls the repetition of the pattern. The default setting is 1, which means the pattern appears once in a 1" x 1" area. If you are hatching small objects, or want a dense pattern, set the scale value to less than 1. In the illustration below, each square was drawn 2" on a side and hatched. The scale for the square on the left is 1, the scale for the square on the right is .125.

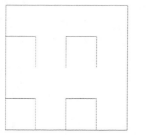 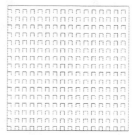

Hatch pattern IUS at a scale of 1 (left) and .125

The Angle field is used to change the angle at which hatch patterns are placed in the drawing. The default value is 0 degrees. If the Crossed option is active, the hatch pattern will be drawn a second time perpendicular to the first pass.

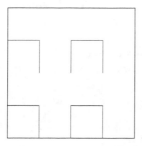 

Hatch pattern IUS at 0 degrees (left) and 45 degrees

You can hatch or fill objects as you draw them, or add hatch/fill to selected objects. Hatches and fills only appear on closed entities.

The complete list of objects that may hold a hatch pattern or a solid color fill is:

- Circle
- Polygon
- Rectangle
- Double line (all modes)
- Closed multiline (single or double)
- Closed spline
- Closed bezier

If using double line to draw a polygon or other closed object, the space between the two lines is hatched or filled, not the interior of the object.

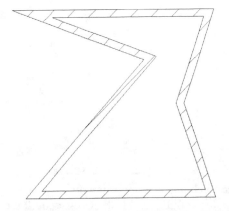

Only the space between the double lines is hatched

To set hatch and fill options before drawing, right-click on the drawing tool you are about to use, select the Brush tab and make your adjustments. To add a hatch or fill to an existing entity, select the entity and select Properties from the local menu (right-click). Click on the Brush tab and adjust the settings as required. A toolbar icon is available for hatch and fill settings; select View|Toolbars|Entity Format from the menu. The settings selected using this tool are used only when the Menu: Format|Create Hatch command is used to hatch selected objects.

Draw with Hatching

Follow the exercise below to gain experience with hatching. You will draw a doubleline polygon with the doubleline hatched one style, and then fill the interior with a second hatch style. To hatch or fill the interior boundary of a doubleline polygon, you will need to trace the interior boundary of the doubleline polygon with the single multiline tool, set with the appropriate hatch details. Finish by drawing an entity without hatching, then select the entity and add hatching.

1. Launch TurboCAD and select the Normal template.

2. Select Double Multiline from the Doubleline flyout toolbar.

Double Multiline tool icon

3. Right-click on the Double Multiline tool to summon the Property Sheet. Click the Brush tab.

4. Set the Pattern to Stars (the sixth item in the list), the color to green and the scale to .5.

NOTE: *You can only set the color in the Brush Property Sheet after you select a hatch pattern. A Hatch setting of None causes the Brush color to revert to the By Pen setting.*

5. Use the Double Multiline tool to draw a closed polygon that fills most of the sheet, similar to the entity shown below. An exact size or shape is not necessary. Before clicking on the point of beginning, right-click and select Close from the local menu.

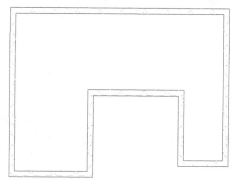

Use Double Multiline to draw a closed polygon

6. Select Multiline from the Line flyout toolbar, then right-click on the tool to summon the Property Sheet. Click on the Brush tab.

7. Set the pattern to L45 (third pattern in the list). Leave the other settings at their defaults.

8. Select Snap Vertex from the Snaps toolbar. Starting at any interior corner, draw a closed polygon by snapping to each interior corner. Before snapping to the point of beginning to finish the polygon, right-click and select Close from the local menu. The new hatch pattern will appear inside the original polygon.

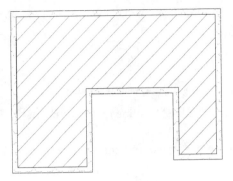

Add hatch pattern L45 to the interior

9. Delete the drawing or save it and start a new drawing.

10. Select Bezier from the Curves flyout toolbar and draw a closed curved that fills most of the sheet, similar to the one shown below. The exact size and shape is not necessary.

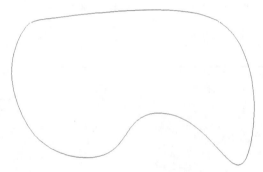

Use Bezier to draw a closed curve

11. Click on the Select tool and select the curve. Right-click and select Properties from the local menu.

12. Click on the Brush tab. Choose any pattern you like; SPANISHTILE is used in the illustration below. Leave scale at 1; color is your choice.

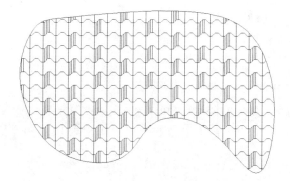

Hatch pattern SPANISHTILE inside the curve

 NOTE: *If a hatch pattern is placed when an entity is originally drawn, TurboCAD considers the hatch to be part of the entity. If a hatch pattern is added later, the hatch is considered a separate entity. In this case you can select the hatch and manipulate it separate from the entity.*

Menu: Format|Create Hatch

An additional option is available to apply hatching or solid fills to entities. From the menu, select Format|Create Hatch to apply a hatch or fill to a selected object. Why use this command instead of just selecting the object and using right-click to adjust the settings in the Brush Property Sheet? If you need to hatch several objects, select all of them, then use the Create Hatch command to hatch them all at once.

The hatch setting you provide when you right-click on a tool is different than the Create Hatch setting. If you need two hatch styles in a drawing, set the tool to one, and Create Hatch to the other. As mentioned above, use the Hatch tool in the Format Entity toolbar to adjust the Create Hatch settings.

Insert a Picture or Object

Hatches and fills are used to embellish geometric entities in TurboCAD drawings, and are useful tools. TurboCAD also allows you to add a wide variety of non-geometric objects to your drawings, using the Insert Picture and Insert Object commands, both found in the Insert menu and the Insert Entity toolbar.

Insert Picture (left) and Insert Object tool icons

Insert Picture is used to place a non-CAD graphic image into a drawing. The command recognizes three graphics formats:

- WMF, Windows Metafile
- BMP, Windows Bitmap
- DIB, Device-Independent Bitmap

To insert a picture into a TurboCAD drawing:

1. Choose Menu: Insert|Picture to display the Insert Picture dialog.
2. Choose the type of graphic file you want to import from the Files of Type drop-down list.
3. If necessary, navigate to the directory or folder where the graphic file you need is stored on disk.
4. Choose the file you want and click the OK button.

TurboCAD uses Windows OLE (Object Linking and Embedding) technology to insert the picture; the picture is an OLE object. You can double-click on the picture and then edit it using Windows Paint (or whatever bitmap editor is registered in your Windows system). Close Paint, and the changes can be seen in the imported image.

Menu: Insert|Picture does *not* establish an OLE link to the original copy of the file you import. If at a later time you use Paint to modify the bitmap picture, those changes will *not* be reflected in your TurboCAD drawing. You can only modify the picture by double-clicking on it from within TurboCAD, or by selecting Edit|Object from the menu. If the picture is selected, you can also access Edit Object from the local menu. The Edit Object command is discussed in the section "Picture and Object edit options" later in this chapter.

TIP: *To select a picture, click along an edge.*

Menu: Insert|Object lets you insert a wide variety of file types into a TurboCAD drawing. The exact list will depend on the software installed on your computer. Insert Object will display every file type listed in your Windows system as capable of OLE actions. Your list should include all these file types:

- AutoCAD drawing (DXF through Version 12, used by most CAD applications).
- Bitmap Image
- Media Clip
- Microsoft ClipArt Gallery
- Microsoft Equation 2.0
- Microsoft Excel 5.0 Chart
- Microsoft Excel 5.0 Worksheet
- Microsoft Excel Chart
- Microsoft Excel Macrosheet
- Microsoft Excel Worksheet
- Microsoft Graph 5.0

- Microsoft Imager 1.0 Picture
- Microsoft Organization Chart 1.0
- Microsoft Word 6.0 Document
- Microsoft Word 6.0 Picture
- Microsoft WordArt 2.0
- MIDI Sequence (sound)
- Microsoft PowerPoint 4.0 Presentation
- Microsoft PowerPoint 4.0 Slide
- Package
- Paintbrush
- TurboCAD 3 (including TurboCAD Designer)
- Video Clip
- WordPad Document (Windows 95)
- Netscape Hypertext Document (HTML)

Consult your application or Windows documentation for descriptions of these file formats and the applications that create them.

Any file added to a TurboCAD drawing using Menu: Insert|Object can be edited from within TurboCAD using the features and commands of the application in which the object was created (called the *source* application). For example, you can insert a Microsoft Excel chart into a drawing and later edit it using Microsoft Excel. Double-click on the chart to establish a link to Excel.

To insert an OLE object into your drawing, select Insert|Object from the menu to display the Insert Object dialog. You can then choose one of two basic options, Create New (the default) or Create From File.

The Create New option lets you embed a new OLE object from another application into your drawing. An example would be if you want to add a spreadsheet chart to your drawing, but have not yet created it. Select the application from the scrolling list and either double-click on the application name or press <Enter>. A selection rectangle will appear as a placeholder for the object, and the source application will run. You can then create the file you need. Exit the source application (you do not need to use the application's Save command), and the object will appear in the drawing. If you select the Display As Icon option, the Windows icon for the application will appear in your drawing instead of the actual bitmap, document, etc. The only way to see the actual file is to double-click on the icon.

 TIP: *Use Display As Icon when you want to add information or other graphics in your drawing, but don't want to clutter the drawing with extra information.*

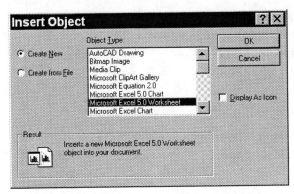

The Create New Version option of the Insert Object dialog

The Create From File option lets you either embed or link an existing OLE object into your drawing. The differences between linking and embedding are important:

- Embedded objects become an integral part of your TurboCAD drawing, and take up more space when saved as a file than a linked object. Embedded objects will move with the file if you transfer it to another computer. If you make subsequent changes to the file on which the embedded OLE object was based, these changes will *not* affect the embedded OLE object in your drawing.

- Linked objects are references to the file on which they were based, and they retain their connection to that file. If you make changes to the file on which a linked OLE object is based, the changes *will* affect the linked OLE object in your drawing.

If you want the object to be displayed only as an icon in your drawing, click the Display As Icon check box.

The Create From File version of the Insert Object dialog

As long as an application program is OLE compliant, a file from it can be linked to your TurboCAD drawings. Let your imagination and creativity run free as you consider possible uses for the Insert Object command:

- An office floor plan could contain a spreadsheet showing the names and serial numbers of every object in the drawing.

- Construction project drawings could contain a video clip showing a 3D "fly-through."

- Mechanical designs could contain charts or statistics showing stress factors, tolerances, etc.

- A series of TurboCAD drawings could be linked to each other.

- A TurboCAD drawing could be linked to a site on the World Wide Web.

- A Microsoft PowerPoint Presentation could be launched from a drawing.

Picture and Object Edit Options

Two commands in the Edit menu can affect pictures and objects you place with Insert Picture and Insert Object. Menu: Edit|Links will display a dialog in which you can make changes to any linked OLE objects in the current drawing. Menu: Edit|Object will allow you to edit a selected OLE object in the object's source application.

 NOTE: *The name of Menu: Edit|Object will change depending on the type of object selected in the drawing.*

The Menu: Edit|Links dialog contains information on every linked object in the drawing. You can use this command to edit the path of a link (if you rearrange your directories and move an application), to force an immediate update of any linked object, or to control when a linked object is updated.

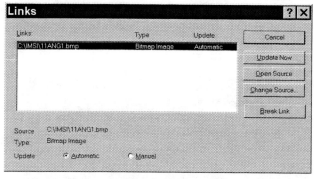

Edit Links dialog

The following functions are available in Menu: Edit|Links:

Update Option. Select either Automatic or Manual to set whether the selected links are updated automatically or only when you request it.

Update Now. This button updates the current link immediately. This is how you update a link if it is set to Manual Update.

Open Source. This button opens the source file in the application that created it. You can compare the linked object to the source file, and make corrections if necessary.

Change Source. This button allows you to change the source application for a linked file.

Break Link. Use this button to change an object from linked to embedded. As explained above, an embedded object will stay with the TurboCAD drawing, but will cause the drawing to be much larger in size when stored on disk.

OLE Drag and Drop

Selected entities or objects can be dragged to a new location in the drawing using the standard Windows drag technique (click and hold the mouse button; move the mouse; let up on the button to place the object in the new location). But if you have another application open side-by-side with TurboCAD, you can drag any selected objects into the other program. This is known as OLE drag and drop.

Windows 95 offers an additional drag and drop method. You can drag an object onto an application's icon in the taskbar. The application will open and accept the object.

Paste Commands

Two commands in the Edit menu, Paste and Paste Special, will insert any data that has been previously copied to the Windows Clipboard. The information could be objects from another TurboCAD drawing, or data from other programs.

Paste is limited to TurboCAD objects, text, bitmaps, and Windows Metafiles.

Paste Special imports any kind of information created by an OLE-compliant application. The list of available file types in the Paste Special dialog depends on the nature of the data in the clipboard. You can choose to have the object link or embed. Once pasted into your drawing, the data behaves as an object placed into the drawing with one of the Insert commands discussed previously.

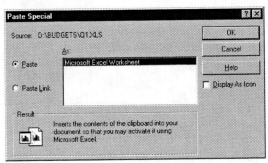

Paste Special dialog

Practice Exercise

Follow the steps below to practice using some of the commands and tools discussed in this chapter. Open the file CH12DET, created in Chapter Seven.

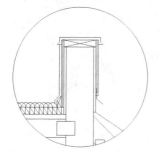 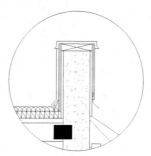

CH12DET.TCW before adding hatch and fill (left) and after

The steps below will guide you through:

- Adding a solid color fill to the rectangle in the lower part of the wall.
- Adding a hatch pattern to the interior of the wall.
- Placing a bit image file in the drawing

This drawing presents an interesting challenge, one that you are ready for if you have worked through the exercises in this book. Because of the various objects used to define the wall, it is not possible to hatch the interior of the wall by simply selecting the boundaries. It will be necessary to trace along the interior. But there are both straight lines and a circle defining the boundaries of the area to be hatched. You will trace using first Multiline, then Arc Center and Radius.

It that weren't enough, once you trace the interior of the wall, you will find it difficult if not impossible to select only the tracings and not the elements of the wall when you try to place the hatch pattern. To get around this problem, you will draw the trace lines on a newly created layer. Then to select the trace lines, you will set all layers to invisible except the layer holding the trace lines. Place the hatch, then restore all invisible layers.

Place Solid Color Fill

1. Select Menu: View|Toolbars, and click on Entity Format, to add the Entity Format toolbar to the desktop

Entity Format toolbar

2. Right-click on the hatch tool in the Entity Format toolbar.

Hatch tool icon

3. Click on the Brush tab.

4. Select SOLID as the pattern, black as the color. Click OK to end.

5. Select the small rectangle near the bottom of the wall. Click on the Hatch tool in the Entity Format toolbar to fill the rectangle.

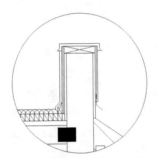

Place a black solid fill in the rectangle

Place Concrete Hatch

6. Right-click on the Hatch tool.

7. Set CONCRETE as the pattern (number 21 in the list), color to gray. Click the Crossed option to select it. Click OK.

8. From the menu, select Tools|Layer. Type "Details" in the name field, and click on New to create an new layer called Details. Click OK.

9. Select the Multiline tool from the Insert Entity toolbar, then right-click on the Multiline tool to summon the Properties dialog. In the General property sheet, select Details as the new layer. Click OK.

10. Select Snap Vertex in the Snaps menu.

11. Use Multiline to trace the interior of the wall, starting at the bottom left where the wall meets the circle. Click on the endpoints that define each corner of the interior, including the intersection of the wall and the circle on the right. Right-click and select Finish from the local menu.

12. Select Arc Center and Radius from the Arc tool in the Insert Entity toolbar. Right-click and set the layer to Details.

13. To define the center of the arc's radius, right-click and select Local Snap|Arc Center from the local menu. Click on the circle.

14. Move the cursor to the lower left corner of the wall, where you started the multiline tracing. Click there to establish the radius, and again to start the arc.

15. Move the cursor to the right and click to finish the arc and close the tracing of the wall.

16. From the menu, select Tools|Layer. Select Details.

17. In Properties, deselect Visible. The "eyes" icon representing a visible layer is removed from Details.

18. Click the Toggle All button. Now Details is set to visible, and all other layers are set to invisible. Click OK.

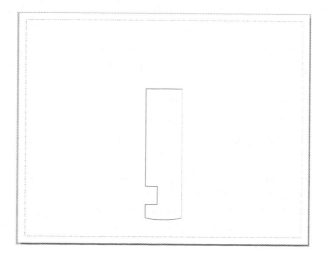

Now only the tracing is visible

19. Use the Select tool to draw a selection rectangle around the tracing. Click on Hatch in the Entity Format toolbar. You will not see any results yet.

20. Select Menu: Tools|Layer again. Select Details, and click the Toggle All button. All other layers will be set to visible again. Click the Visible button to set Details as visible, too.

21. The complete drawing returns to the screen, including a concrete hatch pattern in the wall.

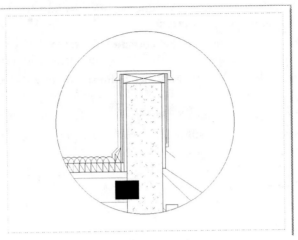

Hatching completed

Insert Bitmap Image

22. Click on Zoom Extents in the View menu.

23. From the menu, select Insert|Object.

24. Leave the default Create New selected. Click on Bitmap Image and click the OK button.

25. A selection rectangle will appear in the drawing, and the Paint program will open. Scratch out a quick doodle, then double-click on the Control Menu box to exit Paint and return to TurboCAD. It is not necessary to save the doodle as a Paint file.

26. Press function key <F5> to redraw the screen. The doodle you created in Paint is now visible in the drawing.

27. Drag the bitmap to any part of the drawing.

28. Save the drawing and exit TurboCAD.

A Wealth of Interconnective Opportunities

The popularity of the Windows operating environment has made it easier for software publishers to allow the import of files created by other programs. TurboCAD takes good advantage of such Windows features as OLE and the Clipboard, allowing you the opportunity to add content created in other programs to your TurboCAD drawings. Data calculated in a spreadsheet, bit-map images from an illustration program, or even video clips are all possible additions to your drawings. The creative possibilities of such links to other "documents" are unlimited.

13

Printing and Plotting

Putting Your Designs on Paper

TurboCAD follows standard Windows protocols for printing, with additional commands in the Page Setup dialog to match the needs of draftsmen and designers.

 Note: In Windows, plotters are treated as printers. If you have a plotter, you need to install special Windows software known as a driver to use it with TurboCAD. If you don't have a driver for your printer or plotter, contact the manufacturer of the device, not Microsoft.

Printer Paper and the Drawing Sheet

As you draw in TurboCAD, you generally see the feature known as the *drawing sheet*. As explained in Chapter Two, the drawing sheet represents Paper Space. The unit of measure in Paper Space matches the units on the sheet you will print to. The drawing sheet can be visible on-screen, yet you can be drawing in World Space (the place where objects are drawn at their real-world size or any scale of it that you prefer).

The drawing sheet is not necessarily the same size as a single sheet of paper that comes out of your printer or plotter. The Drawing Sheet is the total surface area on which your drawing can be printed. The Drawing Sheet can correspond to a single sheet of paper in the printer, or it can span multiple sheets of printer paper.

Both the printer paper and the drawing sheet have adjustable sizes, as well as landscape (wide) and portrait (tall) orientations. This provides a great deal of flexibility when you want to print a large drawing on multiple sheets. You could, for example, print a poster in landscape orientation three feet wide and two feet tall. You could print this virtual sheet out on 32 sheets of 8.5" x 11" paper oriented in portrait, or on 30 sheets of the same size paper oriented in landscape.

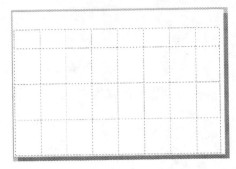

5' x 3' landscape drawing sheet on 8.5" x 11" portrait printer paper

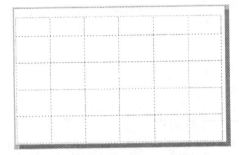

5' x 3' landscape drawing sheet on 8.5" x 11" landscape printer paper

Simple Printing

TurboCAD makes it easy to print in a few simple steps. If you have a drawing created in World Space, and want to print it to one sheet of paper without regard to scale, follow these steps:

1.   Choose Menu: File|Print. The Print dialog will appear.

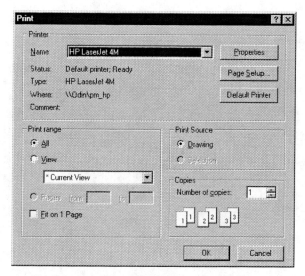

Print Dialog

2. In the Print Range control group, click the All option to print your entire drawing.

3. Check the Fit on One Page option.

4. Click the Page Setup button to bring up the Page Setup Dialog. Choose your printer, paper size, and paper orientation, then click OK to return to the Print dialog.

5. Click the OK button to print your drawing.

Your drawing will be centered and printed on a single sheet of paper.

Tiled Printing

TurboCAD gives you two different approaches to printing a drawing on multiple tiled sheets of paper, using the Paper and Layout property pages of the Page Setup dialog. The two following sections describe these two options.

 Tip: When printing on multiple tiled sheets, it is usually best to have the Print Crop Marks option on, unless you can set your margins to zero. (Not all printing devices can accept zero margins.) Crop marks will enable you to easily trim the edges of the paper so that the sheets can be pasted onto a backing for display.

Tiled Printing by Setting Sheet Size

If you want to create a printout of a specific size tiled on multiple sheets, you can specify the size of the printout in the Paper property sheet. TurboCAD will determine the number and arrangement of the sheets of printer paper.

1. Choose Menu: File|Page Setup. The Paper property sheet will be visible in front.

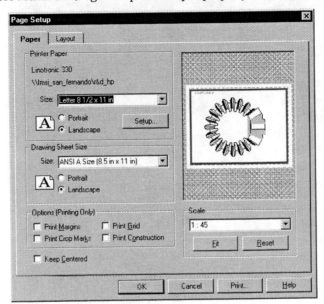

Paper property sheet of Page Setup dialog

2. In the Printer Paper control group, specify the size of the sheets of paper that you want to print on and whether you want to print in landscape (wide) or portrait (tall).

3. In the Sheet Size control group, specify the size of the area on which you want to print the drawing and its orientation. You can do this in any units listed in the Menu: Tools|Units and Scale property sheet. For example, if you want a printout 2 feet tall and 3 feet wide, you would type 2 ft. x 3 ft. in the list box, and choose the Landscape option.

4. Click the Fit button to place your drawing on the tiled sheets.

5. Click the Print button to print your drawing immediately, or click OK and then choose Menu: File|Print if you want to go through the Print dialog.

 Note: *You can also set the sheet size in either World or Page units by specifying values in the Height and Width fields on the Layout property sheet.*

Tiled Printing by Setting Rows and Columns

In the Layout property sheet of the Page Setup dialog, you can specify the number of rows (the number of sheets of printed paper from top to bottom) and columns (the number of sheets of printed paper from left to right). You can then return to the Paper property sheet to fit your drawing onto the tiled printer paper. TurboCAD will automatically adjust the dimensions of the drawing sheet to accommodate changes in the number of rows and columns.

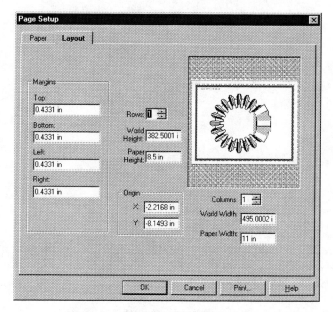

Layout property sheet of Page Setup dialog

Print Commands in the File menu

The following sections discuss each feature available in the File menu for printing and plotting.

Page Setup Dialog

The Page Setup dialog provides a rich set of features that let you determine exactly how drawings will be printed. It consists of a minimum of two property sheets: Paper and Layout. For some printers, additional property sheets are required for advanced features.

 Tip: *After you have selected options in these property sheets, you can either make the changes in your drawing by clicking the OK button at the bottom of the dialog, or print the drawing from the dialog without making changes in your drawing by clicking the Print button. If you click the OK button, you can then print the drawing by choosing Menu: File|Print or clicking the Print button on the Standard toolbar.*

Paper Property Sheet

The Paper property sheet lets you determine the size and orientation of the printer paper and the drawing sheet.

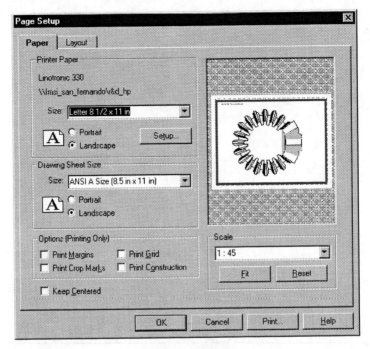

Paper property sheet

Printer Paper

The printer paper is the physical paper that goes through the printer; the drawing sheet is the area on which your drawing will be printed, which can span multiple sheets of printer paper. This property sheet also contains a variety of option controls and a function for viewing or setting the scale of the drawing.

The Printer Paper control group lets you set the size and orientation of the printer paper. These are the same settings you can control through the Print Setup dialog, so changes that you make in this dialog will be reflected in Print Setup, and vice versa. To set the paper size and orientation:

1. Click in the Size list box and choose a standard paper size.

2. Choose either portrait or landscape orientation by clicking one of the option buttons. The icon to the left of the option buttons will change to reflect your choice.

Clicking the Setup button in this control group brings up the Print Setup dialog, in which you can choose another printer or access functions that directly control your printer. This dialog is specific to your printer driver. Check your printer or printer driver documentation for details.

Drawing Sheet Size

The Drawing Sheet Size control group lets you control the size and orientation of the area on which your drawing will be printed. This area can be imposed on a single sheet of printer paper, or it can span multiple sheets of printer paper. Its orientation can also be set separately from the orientation of the printer paper. To set the size and orientation of the drawing sheet:

1. Click in the Size list box and choose a standard paper size, or type in a custom size using standard measurements (for example, 2 ft. x 2 ft.).

2. Choose either portrait or landscape orientation by clicking one of the option buttons. The icon to the left of the option buttons will change to reflect your choice.

The page display on the right side of the dialog will change to reflect the relationship between printer paper and drawing sheet size and orientation.

Options (Printing Only)

The buttons in the Options (Printing Only) control group let you determine what elements are printed. These options affect only the printing of the drawing and are not reflected in the appearance of the drawing on-screen.

Print margins. Check this button to print a border on the margin of the printer sheets. This is useful for framing the drawing if it is printed on a single sheet.

Print crop marks. Check this option button to print crop marks on the printer sheets. This is useful if you want to print across multiple printer sheets and crop the sheets so that they can be pasted against a backing.

Print grid. Check this option if you want to print grid marks. The grid will be printed if it is currently displayed.

Print construction. Check this option if you want to print construction lines.

Page Layout Scale

The controls in the Scale control group let you scale the drawing so that it fits within the drawing sheet, or lets you choose a custom scale.

To scale the drawing so that it fits into the drawing sheet, click the Fit button. The drawing will be centered as it is fit onto the drawing sheet.

To choose a custom scale, click in the list box and choose a preset scale, or type a scale directly into the list box in the form 1 in = 1 ft. When typing custom scales, you can use any measurement available in the Units and Scale property sheet of the Drawing Setup dialog (from the menu select Tools|Drawing Setup). You can click the Reset button at any time to return to the scale that was set when you entered the Page Layout dialog. Drawing Setup is also discussed in Chapter 3, under the heading Preparation For Drawing.

Keep Centered

Check the Keep Centered option to keep the drawing centered over the drawing sheet.

Layout Property Sheet

The Layout property sheet gives you direct control of the number of rows and columns of printer paper. It also has functions for setting the printer paper margins, setting the height and width of the drawing sheet in either World or Paper units, and relocating the paper in the drawing area.

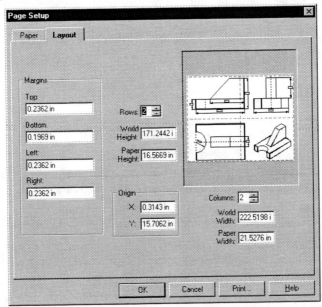

Layout property sheet of Page Setup dialog

Margins

Margins, the dotted rectangle inside the edges of the paper, let you know whether you are drawing inside or outside the printable area of your drawing.

The margins control group contains four text boxes in which you can specify the top, bottom, left, and right margins of the printer paper in Paper units. By default, the margins are displayed in units set in the Units and Scale property sheet (Menu: Tools|Drawing Setup), but you can enter values in other units as well.

 Note: You cannot set the margins of the drawing sheet independently of the margins of the printer paper.

Tip: If you set all the margins to zero, TurboCAD will offer to set them back to give you the biggest possible printable area on the current printer.

Rows and Columns

The Rows and Columns controls let you set the number of rows and columns of the printer sheet paper, for tiled printing. As you increase the number of rows and columns, the size of the drawing sheet — the area on which your drawing will be printed — increases correspondingly. The Paper Height and Paper Width controls let you directly set the height and width of the drawing sheet. As you increase these values, TurboCAD will automatically increase the number of rows and columns to accommodate the change in the drawing sheet size.

Origin

The Origin boxes let you move the paper to a different location in the drawing. You do this by specifying the location of the lower-left corner of the paper in absolute coordinates: Type the horizontal coordinates into the X box and the vertical coordinates into the Y box.

 Tip: This feature is useful if you want to print a particular area of a large drawing by relocating the paper to the area that you want to print.

Print Dialog

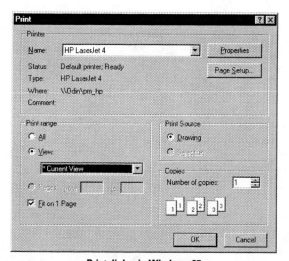

Print dialog in Windows 95

The Print dialog (Menu: File|Print or <Ctrl> + <P>) provides a set of functions which include printing a single view of a drawing, or printing specific sheets in a drawing that spans multiple sheets of printer paper.

Print Source

The Print Source control group lets you choose whether to print all of the drawing objects, or only those that are currently selected.

Print Range

There are times when you will only need to print a portion of a drawing that would span several pages when printed in its entirety. Use the features of the Print Range group to set a specific view of the drawing to print, and to select a range of pages when printing a drawing that spans multiple printed sheets.

All. Select this option if you want to print all of the current drawing. If you have chosen Selection in the Print Source control group, only objects that are selected will be printed. (If your drawing spans multiple printer sheets, the total number of sheets will be shown in this option label.

View. This option allows you to select a Named View, if one exists in the drawing.

Fit on 1 page. Check this box if you want to print everything on a single page.

Copies

Type the number of copies of the drawing that you want to print in the copies text box.

14

Drawing Import and Export

Using Design Files in a Mixed Environment

Sooner or later, you will need to share a TurboCAD drawing with a non-TurboCAD user. The drawing may be headed for desktop publishing, a plotter service, or even another CAD program. Almost every graphics program has its own file format, and translation from one format to another can often become complicated and frustrating. The more you know about the major graphic file formats, the better chance of success you will have when you need to translate your TurboCAD drawings.

This chapter discusses the variety of file formats that you are likely to encounter as a TurboCAD user. The list includes formats used by previous versions of TurboCAD, and file formats used by other CAD programs.

File formats created by bit-image (raster) software is not included in this chapter. For details on using bit-image graphics as objects in a TurboCAD drawing, refer back to Chapter Twelve.

TurboCAD proprietary formats

TurboCAD is no different from every other drawing program on the market, it uses a proprietary format to store the images you create. If you Save a drawing without specifying an alternative file format, the drawing is saved in the .TCW format, short for TurboCAD Windows.

Every new release of a software program offers new features. Some features are obvious to the user, others are buried beneath the surface. It is common practice for software companies to revise the internal workings of how programs store information in files, for a variety of reasons. The publisher may wish to improve the speed at which drawings are saved to disk, to decrease the space required to store a drawing, or to accommodate a new type of data structure in the program (such as moving beyond using only single lines to using multilines).

As TurboCAD has matured over the years, the publishers have found it necessary to make changes to the proprietary file format the program uses to store drawings on disk. To accommodate loyal users who have upgraded from previous versions of TurboCAD, the current version can import the following file formats created by previous versions of TurboCAD:

File Extension	TurboCAD Version or Special Format
TCD	TurboCAD for DOS
TCW	TurboCAD for Windows Version 2
SLW	TurboCAD for Windows Version 2 Symbol Library

To open a drawing saved in one of these earlier TurboCAD file formats, select the correct file format from the Files of Type list box in the Open dialog.

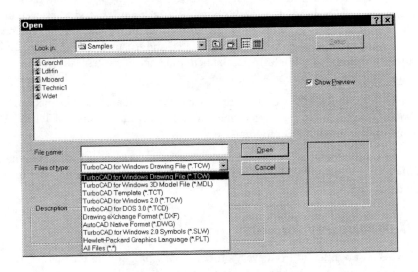

Open dialog showing file format options

Drawing Exchange Format -- DXF

DXF is a file format created by Autodesk, Inc., makers of AutoCAD. This format has become the standard file exchange type for CAD drawings. Virtually every CAD program on the market can read this format. It is usually your best bet if you need to share drawings with the user of another CAD program. DXF will generally preserve your layer definitions, line types and line colors as you created them.

To save a TurboCAD drawing in DXF format, select Menu: File|Save As, then select DXF from the *Save As Type:* list box.

Improving the Readability of DXF files

DXF is widely accepted, but has its limitations. The format does not support the use of solid color fills and hatch patterns. Also, DXF does not support the use of TrueType fonts, which spells trouble for any Windows-based CAD program, including TurboCAD.

There are steps you can take to improve the readability of your drawings when converting them to DXF. Make sure you completely finish the drawing before you create a DXF version. Always keep an original version of the completed drawing in TurboCAD's TCW format. Use the Menu: File|Save As command to create a second copy of the drawing (with a different name), which you will modify before translating to DXF.

Use Menu: Format|Explode to reduce complex elements to basic entities. Your goal is to create a drawing of simple lines, with no complex elements. You should explode all hatch patterns, color fills and lines of text until they are polylines. Explode all groups and blocks to their original constituent parts. Depending on the complexity of the drawing, you may have to explode some elements three or four times before you reduce these elements to simple entities. TurboCAD can only explode one complex object at a time. If you have a large drawing with many elements to explode, you should consider downloading via the Internet a TurboCAD script that automatically explodes every complex element in a drawing. There are two versions, ExpAll32.BAS for the 32-bit version of TurboCAD 3, and ExpAll16.BAS for the 16-bit version. This script, and others, are available on the Internet at http://www.imsisoft.com. From the home page, follow the links to the TurboCAD Sources Forum, and from there to the software library.

TIP: *You can improve the performance of any TurboCAD script if you first remove the Property toolbar from the desktop.*

DWG: AutoCAD native file format

In addition to DXF, TurboCAD can save drawings in AutoCAD's native DWG format. TurboCAD supports the DWG format as used by AutoCAD Release 12. Most earlier version of AutoCAD as far back as Release 9 should also be able to import DWG files created by TurboCAD.

The guidelines provided above for creating reliable DXF files also apply to DWG files.

HP-GL and HP-GL/2: Hewlett Packard Graphics Language

The DXF and DWG formats are best used when sharing your drawings with another CAD user. If you need to send drawings to a plotting service, you will most likely need to translate your drawing to either HP-GL or HP-GL/2, the most common plotter file formats. Before you start the translation, find out if there is a plotter driver for your version of Windows that is an exact match for the plotting device. If so, install it into your version of Windows.

HP-GL is a popular graphics format that is used by both vector and raster graphics programs. HP-GL/2 is an updated version. The language was originally created as a set of codes to send graphics images to Hewlett Packard pen plotters.

TurboCAD 3 for Windows can open an HP-GL file from the Open menu, but does not directly support saving files in either HP-GL format. This is because the correct way to create an HP-GL file is via a program's printing or plotting procedures.

Given the same original drawing, HP-GL files are usually smaller than DXF files. Solid color fills and hatch patterns should translate successfully, but you will still need to explode any text in the drawing. If your plotting service does not give you a specific driver, you must install one of the resident plotter drivers in Windows. For HP-GL, install the HP 7475A; for HP-GL2, select one of the HP Draftmaster plotter drivers. For instructions on installing plotter drivers, consult your Windows documentation. You will select FILE as the destination, not a serial or parallel port. Be sure to use the extension .PLT when you name the file; most programs that can read HP-GL or HP-GL/2 files expect to find the .PLT extension. When you "print" to the plotter device, you create a file on your hard drive; this is the file you will give to your service bureau or otherwise pass along. It is not necessary to have a plotter attached to your computer to use the corresponding Windows driver.

Third-party program for file conversion

Many CAD users have found a shareware program called PrintGL to be of benefit when translating files. PrintGL is a pen plotter emulator package for DOS and Windows. It reads and displays HP-GL and HP-GL/2 data from CAD and graphing packages. It supports a wide variety of 9- and 24-pin printers, ink jet and laser printers. It can export PLT files to PostScript (EPS or device files), and to PCX (Paintbrush) format. You may modify some elements of the PLT file in PrintGL, such as specifying colors or adjusting line types. Another good use of PrintGL is to view PLT files you have created from your TurboCAD drawing, before you pass them along. Some CAD users prefer to use PrintGL as a printer driver, instead of relying on the drivers provided with Windows. This is especially true if you must rely on the HP7475A driver, which has documented problems. PrintGL is available for download on the Internet at http://www.shareware.com, on CompuServe in the Graphics Support Forum Library, and on the Ravitz Software BBS at 606-268-0577. IMSI does not endorse PrintGL, and can provide no support if you use it.

Exporting TurboCAD Drawings Using OLE Drag and Drop

Any Windows program that supports standard Windows Object Linking and Embedding (OLE) can accept a TurboCAD drawing. Open both programs side-by-side. Click on the drawing's reference handle and drag the drawing into the second program. A second method is to Cut or Copy the drawing or selected elements to the Windows clipboard, then use the Paste command in the second program. OLE is described in more detail in Chapter Twelve.

Index

Alphabetical Guide to Topics and Key Words